# Presumed Curable

An illustrated casebook of
Victorian psychiatric patients
in Bethlem Hospital

Sponsored by an educational grant from

# Presumed Curable

An illustrated casebook of
Victorian psychiatric patients
in Bethlem Hospital

**Colin Gale**

Senior Archivist,
Bethlem Royal Hospital Archives and Museum,
Beckenham, Kent BR3 3BX

and

**Robert Howard**

Professor of Old Age Psychiatry,
Institute of Psychiatry, and
Consultant Psychiatrist, Maudsley Hospital,
London SE5 8AF

Wrightson Biomedical Publishing Ltd

Petersfield, UK and Philadelphia, USA

The picture on the cover is of Theodora Weston, who was admitted to Bethlem Hospital as a patient in 1894.

Editorial Office:

Wrightson Biomedical Publishing Ltd
Ash Barn House, Winchester Road, Stroud,
Petersfield, Hampshire GU32 3PN, UK
*Telephone:* 44 (0)1730 265647
*Fax:* 44 (0)1730 260368
*E-mail:* wrightson.biomed@virgin.net

**British Library Cataloguing in Publication Data**
A catalogue record for this book is available from the British Library

**Library of Congress Cataloging in Publication Data**
A catalog record for this book is available from the Library of Congress

ISBN 1 871816 48 3

Design by John Maggs Design, Bath
Composition by Scribe Design, Gillingham, Kent
Printed in Great Britain by Biddles Ltd, Guildford

# Preface

The study of the history of medicine, and especially that of psychiatry, often induces in the modern reader an understandable sense of relief that he or she is living in today's world, and not at any point in the past. Yet the stories of the patients in this book, representatives of many hundreds admitted to Bethlem Hospital in the late Victorian period, will resonate with all who take an interest in mental health care today. In these early years of our own twenty-first century, the fear and stigma associated with major mental illness remain strong. Psychiatrists and professionals in allied disciplines involved in the care and treatment of people with mental health problems still face disorders of uncertain aetiology that devastate the lives of sufferers and their families and for which there are no 'cures'.

The advent of effective treatments for mood disorders and the symptoms of psychosis, some fifty years after the events detailed in this book, did of course result in tremendous improvements in prognosis and the alleviation of suffering. The nineteenth-century casebooks of Bethlem Hospital give relatively little information about the physical and chemical treatments applied to individual patients. Of course, the fact that Bethlem's clinical note-takers did not usually consider drug treatments worthy of mention does not mean that these were never employed. It may, however, suggest that the hospital principally relied

Bethlem Royal Hospital in the early twentieth century.

upon careful maintenance of a therapeutic environment, as glimpsed from time to time in the records, to assist in patients' recovery. It is instructive, and sometimes movingly impressive, to consider what the environment of an institution like Victorian Bethlem could achieve. While writing this book, we have often wondered how different the lives of its patients might have been, had modern drug treatments been available at the time. Cases that would most clearly attract a contemporary diagnosis of schizophrenia, or in which a strong psychotic element accompanied affective disorder – then among the most intractable – would be obvious candidates for recovery today. Twenty-first century medicine might have spared many of the people featured in this book a lifetime of institutionalisation.

But, just as we should not be too quick to dismiss a treatment regimen that resulted in a claimed recovery rate of up to 50%, we should also not complacently assume that we have all the answers today. Development of more effective and acceptable drug treatments for psychosis is an important milestone on a very long and difficult road. Such advances will need to be accompanied by the kind of wholehearted delivery of care aspired to in Bethlem over a century ago if society is to gain the true benefit of everything that has changed for the better in psychiatry in the intervening years.

COLIN GALE and ROBERT HOWARD
*August 2002*

# Acknowledgements

We are grateful to Patricia Allderidge, Archivist and Curator at Bethlem Royal Hospital since 1967, for inspiring and encouraging our study of patient casebooks and photographs. We would also like to thank Dr Dinshaw Master, Stuart Bell and the members of the South London and Maudsley NHS Trust Board for permission to reproduce photographic and case history material. Ian and Angela Moor of the Centre for Photographic Conservation and Geremy Butler of Geremy Butler Photography supplied sympathetic and outstanding conservation and photographic services to the project. We would like to thank our publisher, Judy Wrightson, for her unwavering faith in the concept of the book and for her guidance and support through final production. Finally, thanks to Janssen-Cilag Ltd for the award of an unrestricted educational grant towards production costs.

# Introduction

# Introduction

*'Historians of English psychiatry have generally assumed that the development of modern institutional psychiatry silenced the voice of the mad.'*[1]

The voices of 'the mad' – some of them, at least – are preserved in the medical casebooks of Bethlem Royal Hospital, founded in London in 1247 as a priory dedicated to St Mary of Bethlehem. The laws of copyright and confidentiality protect them from prurient exploitation, but do not silence them. We have distilled a selection of the stories of these patients from the late Victorian medical casebooks of Bethlem Hospital. Within the casebook entries we have chosen, the patients' voices are sometimes indirectly heard through the contents of doctors' certificates (which we have reproduced in full) and clinical records (which we have summarised). More interesting to us have been the direct reports of their speech, their letters – as well as those from their relatives and friends – and of course their extraordinary photographic images. Their voices speak not only of personal mental distress, but of life outside the Hospital, family relationships, and the attitudes and therapeutic régime of a late Victorian psychiatric institution. And each photograph is a window onto a unique human story.

The cases appear in chronological order of admission from 1886 to 1895. Our selection of sixty-one cases is meant to be illustrative, rather than epidemiologically valid. They broadly reflect Victorian Bethlem's slightly higher number of female admissions, and the claimed recovery rate of up to 50% of admissions.[2] At any one point between 1886 and 1895 there were around two hundred and fifty patients in the Hospital, cared for by approximately seventy attendants, or nursing staff.

Under the Lunacy Act of 1845, to which Bethlem became subject in 1853, prospective patients had to be certified insane by two independent doctors. These certificates were subsequently copied into the Hospital's casebooks. Admissions were confirmed (and occasionally refused) by a committee of Hospital Governors within a week of a patient's reception. Details of the physical state, mental condition and previous history of each patient were also entered in the casebooks. Progress notes were added at regular intervals, and from time to time letters, charts and photographs were pasted in. These notes were written by medical staff: the Physician Superintendent, who ran the Hospital on behalf of its Governors, the assistant medical officers who deputised for him, or resident students (renamed clinical assistants in 1889), who spent a year or so at Bethlem as part of their medical training.

Our ambition in putting the stories of Bethlem patients before a wider audience is best expressed in the words of the historian Janet McCalman concerning the subjects of her own research:

*'We have restored them to posterity so that we can share their lives and learn their lessons. We have made their lives count for the future, not be lost and forever forgotten.'*[3]

The voices of these patients deserve to be heard.

## Presumed to be curable

*'All persons of unsound mind, presumed to be curable, are eligible for admission into this hospital for maintenance and medical treatment.'*
(Taken from the regulations printed on the admission forms used by Bethlem Royal Hospital from 1867 to 1906.)

A very clear notion of the kind of patient that Bethlem regarded itself best placed to help is reflected in the Hospital's late Victorian admission regulations. Patients would preferably be 'of the educated classes', although those considered to have 'sufficient means for their suitable maintenance in a private asylum' were not admitted. 'Pauper lunatics', for whom the Hospital had catered for many centuries, were regarded as 'proper objects for admission into a County Lunatic Asylum', rather than as suitable candidates for treatment at Bethlem, by the last quarter of the nineteenth century. In addition, patients were required to present no undue challenge to the Hospital with respect to their physical health. Any whose condition threatened 'the speedy dissolution of life' or who required 'the permanent and exclusive attendance of a nurse' were excluded. Above all, patients had to be curable. Those who had been 'insane for more than twelve months, and are considered by the Resident Physician to be incurable' or who were 'in a state of idiocy, or subject to epileptic fits' were unwelcome. Furthermore, almost all those who showed no signs of recovery after twelve months' residence were discharged uncured as soon as their families could make alternative arrangements for their care.

Alternative arrangements sometimes meant the return of patients to their homes, particularly in those cases in which the families of patients insisted upon discharge against the advice of the Hospital. But more often it meant transfer, either to private institutions (many of which were licensed to admit paupers) or to the very county lunatic asylums that patients had been sent to Bethlem to avoid.

The airing court, or exercise yard, for female patients at Bethlem in the late nineteenth (or early twentieth) century.

Bethlem's restrictive admission criteria had changed little from 1815, when the Hospital relocated from Moorfields to St George's Fields, Southwark (the site of the present-day Imperial War Museum), through to 1948 and the advent of the National Health Service. They reflected a long-standing commitment on the part of this ancient Hospital to short-stay, curable cases. Bethlem did, however, admit a small number of cases to separate 'incurable' wards, but these came only from among its own patient population. Even in these wards, however, treatment continued to be offered with measured optimism, and patients were observed for signs of recovery. According to the Resident Physician's report of 1854, the Hospital Governors did not actually consider that the condition of so-called incurable patients was 'necessarily of so confirmed and hopeless a character as to render them without doubt "incurable"'. There was, or should have been, no way in to Bethlem Hospital for cases considered hopeless.

Occasionally both the physical and mental condition of patients admitted to Bethlem deteriorated beyond reasonable hope of recovery. The Victorian diagnosis for many of these cases, 'general paresis (or paralysis) of the insane', amounted to an admission of how little they were understood.[4] A link between some of the symptoms associated with 'GPI' and syphilis was suspected by the late nineteenth century, but not proven until the early twentieth, and the first effective treatment did not reach Bethlem until the mid-1920s. Generally speaking, patients in terminal neurosyphilitic decline were not discharged from late Victorian Bethlem. Instead, they were cared for through to death, partly out of compassionate loyalty, but also in the interests of medical research. 'These cases would not be admitted if the Committee acted strictly within the limits of the [admission] regulations,' wrote Dr Savage, Physician Superintendent from 1878 to 1888, in Bethlem's annual report for 1883, '...but as I have no desire simply to admit patients for the sake of the appearance of the statistics, so I should be sorry to reject cases in whom the symptoms may be alleviated, although cure is hopeless. General paralysis of the insane must still be looked upon as the one incurable and fatal form of insanity, and if it be not studied in a hospital like Bethlem, which is essentially a hospital for cure and alleviation, I do not see much prospect of its future relief.'

## Governesses, clergymen, medical men, clerks

The one significant development in admissions to Bethlem Hospital in the Victorian era had been a mid-century shift away from admitting paupers (for whom the new county lunatic asylums were thought to cater) in favour of patients of the middle and skilled labouring classes, such as 'governesses, clergymen, medical men, clerks and mech-anics ...'. 'To each of these', wrote Bethlem's Resident Physician, Dr Charles Hood, in 1860, 'the association of a County Asylum would have been painful'. But 'in Bethlem such feelings are spared them: and on leaving these gates they return to their families, their neighbourhood, and their occupation, with their small savings untouched, their social pride unabashed, their gratitude unalloyed.'

In addition, as had been noted in the Hospital's annual report for 1846, 'many of the better class of patients do ultimately appreciate very highly the benefits they receive' by their treat-ment, and their 'expressions of sincere gratitude' pleased the hardworking Hospital staff.

Through their powers of veto over applications for admission to the Hospital, Hood's successors deliberately increased the numbers of middle and lower middle class (as opposed to pauper) patients at Bethlem throughout the 1860s and 1870s. In 1881, this policy received a boost from a decision by the Charity Commission to allow Bethlem to admit paying patients in addition to its ordinary, non-paying patients. Prior to this, patients (or their relatives or friends) had not paid anything to the Hospital other than a bond (set high at £100 at this time, though lowered in 1883) to be returned upon discharge.

From 1882 onwards, patients' relatives who were willing to pay to secure a place at Bethlem contributed two guineas a week towards the cost of care, but paid no bond. To a certain extent, this new provision must have been motivated by a desire to keep the

A male ward at Bethlem Hospital, as it appeared in *The Illustrated London News* in 1860. The central, sideburned figure could possibly be Dr Charles Hood, Physician Superintendent from 1852 to 1862.

Hospital full in order to help meet its overheads. But its effect was to further sway the social composition of the patient population in favour of members of the kind of families who were anxious (and prepared to pay a little) to maintain their social respectability, but who were unable to afford the high cost of private care.

In 1886, Bethlem began to admit a small number of 'voluntary boarders', who were not certified insane, but who wished admission for treatment. In place of medical certificates, signed declarations from the prospective patient and a responsible friend or relative were required for admission. Such patients could change their minds and discharge themselves after giving seventy-two hours' notice, at least for as long as they remained uncertified. It was not uncommon, however, for patients to enter the Hospital as voluntary boarders, become certified at an early stage of their residence and be technically re-admitted as ordinary patients. The proportion of voluntary admissions to Bethlem increased in the decades that followed, encouraged by provisions in the amended 1890 Lunacy Act, and the 1930 Mental Treatment Act. In the 1920s, *The Lancet* expressed the view of the 'average man' that 'a patient must be very insane indeed if he were of his own free will to seek admission'.[5] The number of voluntary admissions to Bethlem, from the late Victorian period onwards, suggests that in fact the environment of the Hospital was not altogether unappealing to those who felt in need of help.

Victorian engravings of Bethlem's interior give an impression of a comfortable, well-lit, almost 'dining club' ward environment. A far cry from the image of its alter-ego, 'Bedlam'. The word 'bedlam' had started out simply as a way of spelling the name of the Hospital (alongside 'Bethlem', 'Bethlehem' and a number of other medieval variants), but had assumed a life of its own thanks to seventeenth and

A female patients' sewing class in the late nineteenth (or early twentieth) century.

eighteenth century dramatists and satirists, until it entered the dictionary as a synonym for confusion and uproar. The nineteenth century witnessed a sustained attempt on the part of the Hospital Governors to shed this image. In particular, the appointment of Dr Charles Hood as Bethlem's first Resident Physician in 1852 coincided with a major shift in the Hospital's approach to mental health treatment. Use of mechanical restraint – manacles, straitjackets, and so on – to control disruptive or violent patients was discontinued in favour of the 'moral management' of patients. The regulation of the patients' environment was a key component of this strategy. Sewing and singing classes, chapel services, lending libraries, airing courts (or exercise yards), gardens, games and sports all had their part to play in the therapeutic régime.

## Polite society

As regulated as Hospital life undoubtedly was, it was not lived entirely in isolation from the outside world. Well-behaved patients were permitted to go on unsupervised walks outside the Hospital walls, and were granted temporary leave of absence (typically at Christmas, and in convalescence). Groups of patients and staff went on organised outings to places such as Kew Gardens, the Crystal Palace, and Brighton Beach. The staff recognised that this approach carried some degree of risk. Dr George Savage, one of Hood's successors (but best known today as one of the doctors in private practice who attended Virginia Woolf), was sanguine about this. In his annual report to the Hospital Governors for 1884, he wrote, 'Risk has to be run, and it is only after long and often painful experience that a physician learns whom to trust and how much, and even with the best experience one may be mistaken'. What he longed to see, as he had explained in the annual report for 1881, was a time 'when it will be the very few, in an asylum such as Bethlem, who will be under lock and key, the others being treated as invalids and nothing more'.

For most patients, the most avidly awaited event on the Hospital's social calendar was the monthly patient dance, to which members of the public were also invited, and at which male and female patients, usually segregated in separate wings of the Hospital, were encouraged to mix. Attendance was a privilege granted upon good behaviour (and withheld upon bad behaviour) by the Resident Physician. The observations of Hospital staff on patients' behaviour at the ball, and the ire of those patients who were denied permission to attend, underline its therapeutic and social significance.

An outsider's account of one of these balls is preserved in a letter written by Thomas Seaton Leadman in March 1883. 'Last Friday I went

The patients' ball at Bethlem, as it appeared in *The Illustrated London News* in 1859.

7

Ticket for admission to the patients' ball, 1886.

to a small dance at "Bedlam" ... It was a most interesting visit, not at all alarming or disagreeable in any way. Most of the inmates are of the middle class order and a few very superior people such as artists and university men. I danced with a little governess who knew four languages ... To talk to she was rather more sane than I am, but when her mania comes on, which is that people are talking about her, she hides her face in her hands and remains so for a couple of days...'. These observations prompted Leadman to surmise that 'monomania' was 'purely an exaggeration of everything we have in our daily life, and sometimes very little coloured indeed'.

The cartoon published in *Punch* in 1882 (pictured below) might give rise to doubt as to whether the receipt of an invitation to a ball at Bethlem always prompted such sympathy for the plight of its patients as shown by Leadman. But perhaps this would be to take its humour too seriously. At least the cartoon demonstrates that such invitations were commonly received by members of polite society, and that mental disorder was thought to be susceptible to treatment.

ONE FOR HIS NOB.

*Cousin Charley (an eminent Dancing Man)*. "JUST FANCY, EDITH! I'M ENGAGED TO GO TO A BALL AT BEDLAM NEXT WEEK!"
*Edith.* "TAKE CARE THEY DON'T KEEP YOU, WHEN ONCE THEY GET YOU, CHARLEY DEAR!"
*Fiendish Rival.* "THEY ONLY TAKE IN THE CURABLE CASES, MISS EDITH!"

No doubt the Hospital issued ball invitations to maintain patients' contact with the outside world, and for its own public relations purposes. Perhaps it had a further aim in doing so: to promote better mental health awareness in society at large. Writing in the Hospital's annual report for 1883, Dr Savage certainly felt that 'insanity can neither be understood properly or fairly dealt with, till the sane people know more about and lose their dread of it'.

## Care and control

Within late Victorian Bethlem, these liberal initiatives for the care of quiet, well-behaved or convalescent patients co-existed with a range of measures that could be applied to control and alter the

Cartoon in *Punch* magazine, 24 June 1882.

behaviour of the less co-operative. After the death of Dr Hood in 1870, there had been a limited return to the temporary use of mechanical restraint to control patients thought to be in a state that was dangerous to themselves or others. The Hospital mostly employed 'strong dresses' with sleeves enclosing the hands of the wearer in padding, 'side arm dresses' with sleeves sewn to the sides of the garment, and 'soft gloves', fastened around the wrists, enclosing the hands in padding. A technique known as 'the dry wrap' was also sometimes used. This involved wrapping patients in a sheet or blanket, then pinning them to a mattress with another sheet fastened under the bed.

The re-introduction of mechanical restraint at Bethlem had its detractors, and became the subject of particular controversy in the letters column of *The Times* in 1888. Dr Savage, about to retire from the post of Physician Superintendent, entered a stout defence. 'I acknowledge no principle of "non-restraint", but only the higher one of humanity and humane treatment, which, if it means anything, means the use of every method to restore health,' he wrote to *The Lancet*. 'There are no straight waistcoats, handcuffs, or what may be called true instruments of restraint in Bethlem; no patients are ever kept quiet by means of drugs, and it is very rare for patients to be held by attendants after the first day or two...'.[6]

The mechanical restraint of patients cannot seriously have been considered remedial. At best it was intended to foil attempts at self-harm, suicide or assault. But the potential for scandal arising from the abuse of restraint was well understood. Detailed records were kept of the use of restraint, and were subject to regular inspection by the government's Commissioners in Lunacy (as was the Hospital itself). Likewise, the force-feeding of patients was a preventative, not a curative, measure. It was limited to those whose lives were considered endangered by their refusal to eat, and carried its own element of risk to patients' health, as well as a degree of controversy.

Even Bethlem's great exponent of 'moral management' and 'non-restraint', Dr Hood, was willing to include a range of chemical and physical treatments within his therapeutic régime. In his report to the Governors for 1853, he cited the instance of Martha Clary, who was brought into the care of the Hospital threatening violence and wearing a straitjacket. She had been freed from her restraint, given a warm bath and two grains of acetate of morphia, and isolated in a padded room overnight. Two days later, when she was calmer, a drop of croton oil was

Dr George Savage, Physician Superintendent from 1878 to 1888.

Dr Percy Smith, Physician Superintendent from 1888 to 1898.

9

administered as a laxative, and the next day henbane was given to combat feverishness. After six weeks Clary was discharged recovered.

Hood's successors were equally enthusiastic advocates of physical treatments. Hydrotherapy, which usually meant bathing patients in warm water for prolonged periods, was a common intervention. Bathing in cold water as shock therapy and placing patients in temporary isolation, or 'seclusion', were also practised.

As for sedative drug treatments, the range of possibilities grew throughout the latter half of the century, with the introduction of bromides in the 1850s, chloral in the 1860s and 1870s, and paraldehyde and hyoscine in the 1880s. To judge from the late Victorian casenotes of Bethlem, the doctors' drug of choice seems to have been hyoscine. In the Hospital's annual report for 1889, Dr Percy Smith, Dr Savage's successor as Physician Superintendent, welcomed the addition of a newly manufactured tranquilliser, sulphanol, to the medical arsenal 'for the production of sleep and the control of excitement', remarking that several patients owed their recovery to its use. It is not clear what had happened to Dr Savage's earlier boast that drugs were never used to keep Bethlem patients quiet. Perhaps Dr Smith would have argued that their effects on mental illness went beyond sedation.

Bethlem depicted as a cage by a patient in the late nineteenth (or early twentieth) century.

## Flitting the cage

Whether the therapeutic régime at Bethlem in the late nineteenth century is regarded as relatively enlightened or harsh partly depends upon whether one attends mainly to the voices of its doctors, or to those of its patients. While the views of its doctors have been quoted in this introduction, the views of its patients are the subject of this book as a whole. Perhaps it is not surprising to find Bethlem depicted as a domed birdcage by a late Victorian or early Edwardian patient.

Very few ever attempted to escape, and fewer still made good their escape. But the precise nature of patients' experiences at Bethlem had much to do with the ward in which they were placed. Patients were sometimes as keen to be transferred from one ward to another as they were to be discharged from the Hospital.

There were four floors in both wings of the Hospital, the lowest numbered I and the highest IV. On each floor galleries, or wide corridors, ran the length of the wings, and patients' rooms opened directly onto these galleries. The galleries formed separate wards except for those in the basement, in which were kept the Hospital's most challenging patients. In an effort to maintain order, these galleries were divided into two in the early 1880s. They were known respectively as MIA and MIB (on the male side) and FIA and FIB (on the female side).

These basement wards became notorious among patients. One of the patients whose case appears in this book claimed in a letter to have received physical and verbal abuse at the hands of attendants on MIB ward. He added gratefully 'I shall ever remember the different treatment that is used towards the patients in No. IV

Bethlem's convalescent establishment at Witley in the early twentieth century.

Gallery'. Upon being transferred from Gallery III to MIB, another patient threatened to assault staff with half a brick unless he was returned. A third was even moved to speculate, in sarcastic verse, as to which ward Dr Savage might occupy after death if heaven was stratified along Bethlem lines.

As often as not, the immediate prelude to patients 'flitting the cage' through their discharge was transfer to Witley, Bethlem's convalescent establishment in rural Surrey. From its opening in 1870 until its closure in 1929, Witley was a much longed-for destination among the patients. Its régime was mild and its environs pleasant, but the chief attraction of transfer there was the associated prospect of imminent departure from Bethlem. It was not uncommon for convalescent patients to be sent to Witley for a month, and – all being well – discharged a day or two after their return to the Hospital. Small wonder then, that Geoffrey O'Donoghue, Bethlem chaplain from 1892 to 1930, and author of *The Story of Bethlehem Hospital from its Foundation in 1247* (published in 1914), once asked rhetorically, 'What is the cheeriest sight in the Hospital?', and answered 'To see some of our friends outside the box-room packing their boxes for Witley'.[7]

## Photography and diagnosis

It has been argued that photography was a 'useful tool of surveillance and control' in the hands of Victorian psychiatrists, criminologists and others, especially in those institutions that needed records to identify

Henry Hering's portrait of Eliza Crapp, a Bethlem patient from 1858 to 1859.

11

inmates.[8] Bethlem Hospital does not seem to have used the camera for this purpose. Photographing patients never became part of its admission procedure. It was done sporadically, and never comprehensively: first by experienced photographers, Henry Hering in the late 1850s and Sir Francis Galton in the early 1880s, and then by a succession of Hospital staff, relative amateurs behind the lens, from the mid-1880s to the mid-1890s.

Henry Hering's motives in photographing Bethlem patients, and Dr Charles Hood's motives in allowing him to do so, are unrecorded. However, the photographs – several dozen of them – may have been used for diagnostic purposes. Lithographic drawings were made of some of them for inclusion in a series of essays on the physiognomy of insanity by Dr John Conolly.[9] A physician with a trained eye, Conolly implied, could read the diagnosis in a patient's face. Dr Hood's own copies of the photographs were (in many cases) placed on individual mounts on which were recorded patients' initials and their diagnoses.[10]

An unmounted print of a Bethlem patient was sold by Hering to Charles Darwin in November 1866. It was subsequently kept by Darwin in a parcel of sources for his *Expression of Emotions in Man and Animals*, in which he argued that the fact that facial expressions are shared by different species suggests a common progenitor.[11] Dr Hood's mounted copy of the print sold to Darwin gives the initials of the female subject as 'E.C.' and her diagnosis as 'acute mania'. Its subject was Eliza Crapp of Castle Street, Reading, admitted to Bethlem aged 65 on 11 June 1858 following the sudden death of her husband, and discharged well fourteen months later. Many of Hering's other subjects can also be identified, and their medical records found. To date, however, there has been little interest shown in putting names to their faces. The photographs may have been used at first for diagnostic purposes. Latterly they have been used as exhibition pieces, or to illustrate a thesis. In each case, the humanity and individuality of the anonymised subjects is lost. Patients have been identified by their initials and diagnosis, or have remained nameless altogether. Supposition and error, which might have been avoided by study of the records of Bethlem Hospital, has at times crept into the critical appreciation of these portraits.[12]

Francis Galton's portrait of Helen Smith, a Bethlem patient in the winter of 1881–82 (reproduced by permission of University College London[14]). Smith returned as a patient in 1888 (see pages 38–39).

The ultimate motivation of Francis Galton in photographing patients at Bethlem Hospital was eugenic rather than diagnostic. He believed that physical and mental affinities and chains of descent could be detected in photographic portraiture, and sought to define racial, criminal, and medical physiognomies by amassing and analysing as many images as he could. To his mind, a thorough grasp of eugenics would throw open the possibility of replacing natural selection as the agent of evolutionary change with benign human intervention: 'what nature does blindly, slowly and ruthlessly, man may do providently, quickly and kindly'.[13]

Why Galton was permitted to photograph Bethlem patients in service of these aims is unknown. The results of his work, approximately 140 head-and-shoulders portraits, may now be seen in University College London's Department of Manuscripts and Rare Books. Many of the patients have large numbers pinned to their clothes. These numbers do not form any part of the Hospital's data on these patients. Evidently they were Galton's own means of identifying his subjects. Titles and surnames of patients (supplied no doubt from a list of names numbered to correspond with those worn by patients) were added in longhand underneath each print. Even so, his images of people identified by number could easily give rise to a false impression of the way patients were treated at Bethlem Hospital.

A page from an album of patient photographs used for teaching purposes at Bethlem Hospital.

Photographs were taken of over three hundred Bethlem patients by Hospital staff from the mid-1880s to the mid-1890s.[15] These include the photographs that illustrate this book. Resident students Alfred Barker and Herbert Parker were the first to do so in earnest in 1888. They were followed by Carbutt Fairbank, Head Attendant from 1891 to 1893, and Horace Pring, clinical assistant from 1894 to 1895. Others may have been involved in taking photographs. If so, their names remain unknown. Though apparently undertaken at the initiative of the individuals concerned, this photography was done in the course of their work at Bethlem. Indeed, in 1892 the Hospital fitted out a darkroom for the use of Mr Fairbank. Prints of many of the photographs were included in an album as well as pasted into patients' medical records. According to a letter written by Dr Smith in 1930, many years after his retirement as Bethlem's Physician Superintendent, the album was intended for use in 'the instruction of students attending at the Hospital'. In it, patients were grouped by diagnosis. Whether medical students ever learnt from it to distinguish at a glance 'melancholia' from 'mania', or 'dementia' from 'general paralysis of the insane', is not recorded.

# Named and famed

Names of patients whose cases and photographs appear in this book have not been changed or otherwise anonymised. The confidentiality of medical records in England and

Wales is protected for one hundred years by regulation. Access is allowed to records older than this. Recent case studies on the institutional care of psychiatric patients have had to anonymise individual histories because much of their data is from the twentieth century.[16] All of the material in this book that is derived from medical records is at least one hundred years old, and not subject to this kind of restriction.

There is, however, a more important reason why we have decided to put the real names of the patients featured in this book alongside their case histories and photographs. We want to rescue their cases from being discussed impassively as no more than examples of Victorian diagnosis and treatment, and their images from being exhibited namelessly as no more than examples of the use to which photography was put by nineteenth century medicine. Something of the patients' individuality is conveyed through these sixty-one stories, even – perhaps especially – through the stories of greatest human distress. Of course, the casenotes do not provide the last word on any of these people. They represent no more than a snapshot taken at a most testing time in their subjects' lives. Even so, real individuals are the subjects of these stories. By giving them their true names, we can correctly attribute their experiences and make them count for something.

Above all, these patients were among the ordinary people of their time. Bethlem Royal Hospital at St George's Fields had its share of residents who achieved celebrity. The likes of Richard Dadd, Antonia White and Louis Wain remain popular subjects of study today. But the people featured in this book are of no less interest as psychiatric patients, and deserve no less attention as human beings. In each of their cases, hope was entertained of their recovery at the time of their admission into Bethlem Royal Hospital, and – whatever may be thought of their treatment – that medical optimism was by no means always disappointed. By attending to the voices of these patients, we can accord them a posthumous dignity that is fully consonant with that hope.

## Notes

[1] Akihito Suzuki, 'Framing Psychiatric Subjectivity: Doctor, patient and record-keeping at Bethlem in the nineteenth century', *Insanity, Institutions and Society, 1800–1914: A Social History of Madness in Comparative Perspective*, edited by Joseph Melling and Bill Forsythe, Routledge, 1999, p. 131. Roy Porter provides a nuanced account of this 'silencing' in 'Hearing the Mad: Communication and Excommunication', *Proceedings of the 1st European Congress on the History of Psychiatry and Mental Health Care*, edited by Leonie de Goei and Joost Vijselaar, Erasmus Publishing, Rotterdam, 1993, pp. 338–352. Medical certificates and casebook entries do not always provide straightforward access to patients' perspectives. But they do contain the raw material from which these perspectives may be recovered.

[2] With respect to the recovery rates claimed by Bethlem in the nineteenth century, it is worth bearing in mind that these related strictly to admissions, rather than to patients. An extreme case illustrates the difference between the two: Florence Wakeley, admitted and discharged recovered or 'relieved' seven times between 1890 and 1902, must have figured in the Hospital's statistics as having recovered not once, but seven times (see pages 52–53).

[3] From Janet McCalman's acceptance speech at the New South Wales Premier's History Awards 1999, available in print in the Australian Society of Archivists' *Bulletin*, October 1999 (no 5), pp. 10–14, and online at: **http://www.asap.unimelb.edu.au/asa/aus-archivists/msg01497.html**. McCalman was awarded the Premier's 1999 Community and Regional History Prize for her book *Sex and Suffering. Women's Health and a Women's Hospital: the Royal Women's Hospital, Melbourne 1856–1996*, Melbourne University Press, 1999.

[4] For a description of the symptoms associated with general paralysis of the insane, see Edward Shorter, *A History of Psychiatry from the Era of the Asylum to the Age of Prozac*, John Wiley & Sons, New York, 1997, pp. 53–59.

[5] *The Lancet* **2** 1924, p. 709, quoted in Jonathan Andrews, Asa Briggs, Roy Porter, Penny Tucker and Keir Waddington, *The History of Bethlem*, Routledge, London, 1997, p. 654.

[6] *The Lancet* **2** 1888, p. 738, quoted in Bethlem Royal Hospital's Annual Report for 1888, p. 38. The controversy is tracked, and biographical details of Dr Savage (and of two other Bethlem doctors, Theophilus Hyslop and Maurice Craig) are given, in Stephen Trombley's *'All That Summer She Was Mad': Virginia Woolf and Her Doctors*, Junction Books, London, 1981. Though Dr Savage entered private practice after his retirement from Bethlem, he maintained close links with the Hospital until his death in 1921. As a lecturer on mental disease at Guy's Hospital, he often illustrated issues of diagnosis by presenting Bethlem patients to his classes of medical students, including at least one featured in this book (see page 75).

[7] *Under the Dome* [Bethlem Royal Hospital magazine], 25 March 1916, page 1.

[8] Elaine Showalter, *The Female Malady: Women, Madness and English Culture, 1830–1980*, Virago, 1987, p. 97, quoting Susan Sontag, *On Photography*, Penguin, 1977.

[9] Published in the *Medical Times and Gazette*, January 1858–February 1859. Extracts from these essays, the prints, and many of the photographs themselves, are reproduced in Adrienne Burrows and Iwan Schumacher's *Portraits of the Insane: The Case of Dr Diamond*, Quartet Books: London, 1990, pp. 85–152. At first, Burrows and Schumacher regarded Hering's portraits as possibly the work of Dr Hugh Diamond, medical superintendent of Surrey County Lunatic Asylum, but they withdrew this suggestion, for which there was simply no support, in the second edition of their work. Nevertheless, their original error has led others astray from time to time. According to Cath Quinn, for instance, the photographs are 'generally assumed to be the work of Diamond' and their subjects regarded as patients, not of Bethlem Hospital, but of Surrey County Lunatic Asylum ('Images and impulses: representations of puerperal insanity and infanticide in late Victorian England' in *Infanticide: Historical Perspectives on Child Murder and Concealment, 1550–2000*, edited by Mark Jackson, Ashgate, Aldershot, 2002, p. 205).

[10] Now held in Bethlem Royal Hospital's Archives & Museum.

[11] Peter Hamilton and Roger Hargreaves, *The Beautiful and the Damned: The creation of identity in nineteenth-century photography*, (Lund Humphries, London, 2001, pp. 73–77. The print in question is now kept among anthropological photographs in the Darwin archive, Cambridge University Library.

[12] An example of error (other than that outlined in note 9 above) is Hamilton and Hargreaves' belief that 'the subjects of Hering's photographs had all been consigned there for violent crimes' (*The Beautiful and the Damned*, p. 82). An example of supposition, albeit concerning the set of photographs taken by Dr Hugh Diamond of patients at Surrey County Lunatic Asylum, is Elaine Showalter's remark that his female subjects' ill-fitting clothes were 'obviously from the hospital store' (*The Female Malady*, p. 87).

[13] Quoted by Ann Thomas in *Beauty of Another Order: Photography in Science*, Yale University Press, 1997, p. 130.

[14] Library Services, Galton Papers 158/2D, female patient No. 9.

[15] These photographs have been on closed access until comparatively recently, and have attracted little by way of scholarly attention (but see Cath Quinn, 'Images and impulses' p. 210).

[16] Geoffrey Reaume, *Remembrance of Patients Past: Patient Life at the Toronto Hospital for the Insane, 1870–1940*, Oxford University Press, Don Mills, Ontario, 2000, and Diana Gittins, *Madness in its Place: Narratives of Severalls Hospital, 1913–1997*, Routledge, London, 1998.

# The Patients

# 'You have systematically and fraudulently ruined my social and commercial position'

Taken on 21 March 1888.

**Walther Wolfram, a 40-year old Austrian Commission agent living in Catford, was admitted on 12 May 1886.**

*He has been under my notice for the last three weeks and has been highly excitable and restless. He has also most exalted and exaggerated ideas about his financial position and says his returns are now £300,000 a year. He buys anything that takes his fancy at random and without regard to cost. He went alone to Brighton on Good Friday and spent all his money on vases, pictures, etc. He gave a cabman his watch for driving him about nearly all night. I fetched him home from Brighton on Easter Monday when he was in the same mental condition and has remained so ever since.*

Dr Henry Wintle, Kingsdown Church Road, Forest Hill

*Mr Wolfram offered to lend me £5000 in a frivolous manner and presses the loan, promising to call with his solicitor and let me have the money tomorrow. He, in a similar way, is willing to lend £5000 to any friend of mine. Walter Simpson tells me that Mr Wolfram bought, at a fair, goods to a large amount of a kind utterly useless for his business and which had to be countermanded by his brother. He told Mr Simpson by letter that he would sell it all in a day. He took a place of business at £500 a year rental, which is utterly useless to him and obviously so. He buys in all directions, extravagant articles and is very violent in rejecting interference with his wild projects.*

Dr Walter Moxon, 6 Finsbury Circus, London

At the time of admission he was known to have had syphilis, and an observed inequality of the size of his pupils and a tremor of his tongue and lips noted by the admitting doctor were consistent with this diagnosis. He spoke quickly and clearly with a 'foreign accent' and although his initial response to conditions in the Hospital was one of disgust, on his second day described the ward as 'quite comfortable' and pronounced the food as 'excellent'. He remained in this state of apparent contentment for most of his time at Bethlem and would occupy himself by playing the piano during the day and whist in the evenings. He kept a diary, the contents of which seem to have been read by the staff. In his diary, he wrote in French of having met a very beautiful young woman in the Hospital chapel who had told him that she was a widow with three children. He also made entries describing a supposed visit that he had made to Downing Street to consult with Ministers, and concerning his plans to set up a benevolent institution for the poor, ill and mentally infirm. A footnote to these reported diary entries is as follows: 'It should be added that the lady he describes as being very beautiful is quite the reverse and has the delusion that she is the mother of the Royal Princes'.

A letter he wrote on 31 August to a fellow patient convalescing at Witley provides a glimpse of a network of communication and friendships among patients. 'Dear old pal!' he greeted his unnamed correspondent. 'Mr Piper [another patient at Witley] wrote to Mr Walters [a patient on Wolfram's ward] that you are well and are enjoying yourself and I can mention the same about me. We are living the same way as before and enjoying ourselves as well as we can. Haider has been removed into No. I, as he was at last unbearable, with his spitting, messing, etc. I hope to get out when Dr Savage is back from his journey. I am completely sick of this life, after I had four months of it. Give my kind regards to Messrs Sedgwick and Piper'. Wolfram appended further brief but telling notes about Hospital life to his letter: 'Smoke as heavy as before but there is good supply of 'bacco and cigars in my case. Today confounded fish dinner. Old Walters here yet. His people seem to be a bad lot and humbug the old fellow terribly. They deserve shooting.'

Wolfram's hopes of an early discharge were dashed, and on 5 October he became very agitated because Dr Savage would not allow him to return to his place of business. He told Dr Savage that he was perfectly capable of managing his business affairs and gave as proof of this the fact that since his admission he had been writing to his partner with instructions as to how he should proceed. The Hospital staff, however, had been opening and reading these letters, the majority of which said 'Send me 2/6 and some cigars'.

He became more physically unwell and by 30 January 1887 it was reported that at the Hospital dances his legs were so weak that he was only able to go halfway around the room without having to stop for a rest. Despite his weakness, he would still 'forget himself' at the dances and was noticed to be taking ladies round the waist with both hands. Nor was his sense of outrage at his continued detention diminished. He vented his spleen in a letter to Dr Savage, dated 6 February, in which he wrote: 'Your insolent and ungentlemanly exhibitions towards me induce me to put the distinct request before you, in future not to take the slightest notice of me, as I emphatically decline any intercourse with you after the scandalous occurrence you provoked last night. Before I was banished to this hell upon earth, my position in social life was to be quite as dignified, if not superior, to the one you hold, and if you were not a medical man, employed in a lunatic asylum, I would demand you to meet me on a very different footing. You have systematically and fraudulently ruined my social and commercial position, and even spoiled my domestic happiness; and you will regret, one day yet, the evil and cruelty which you have committed to a respectable man'.

He was visited by the Austrian Consul on 15 April 1887, but continued his physical and mental decline. His behaviour became more unpredictable and difficult to manage, and his relationships with fellow patients more acrimonious – if the exchange between himself and Arthur Postans reported in Postans' medical notes (see page 45) is a reliable guide. On 5 June 1889 Wolfram was sent down to MIB ward because he had been spitting mucus around the ward (perhaps in emulation of Haider, the patient mentioned in the letter he wrote three years earlier), and on 3 March he destroyed a sofa because he believed his father was hidden inside it. Through 1889 and 1890 he was described as 'tottering and weak' and was subject to convulsions. He was nursed on a waterbed to prevent development of bedsores, and died on 3 December 1890.

## 'That man will fix in a madhouse'

Taken on 24 March 1888.

**Ernest Woodward, a 33-year old estate agent from Bedfordshire, was admitted on 16 December 1886.**

*He says he is the Emperor of Russia. That he is the strongest and richest man in the world. That the Millennium begins on the first of January. John Gallin states that he is constantly talking incoherently.*

Dr Ethelbert Hosking, Turner's Hill, Sussex

*Says he can cure all the sick people in the world in a day by touching them. Calls himself Emperor of Russia, Earl of Cleveland and the True Prophet. Threatens to kill all people who dare to contradict him. His wife, Mary Woodward, tells me that he uses disgusting language and is constantly swearing, such not being his habit previous to the present attack. He constantly talks to himself and does not know where he is.*

Dr Percy Evershed Wallis, Old Stone House, East Grinstead, Sussex

His symptoms were thought to have begun in February 1886 when he had developed hypochondriacal depression and had been unable to work. In November he had started to express grandiose ideas and had experienced visual hallucinations, seeing visions of angels and Jacob's Ladder. Shortly after Woodward's admission, Dr W. Johns of March, Cambridgeshire wrote to the Physician Superintendent that 'Mr Woodward contracted syphilis, as near as I can remember, in 1878. He had well marked secondary symptoms but did not seem to suffer much in general health. I am inclined to think that his mental derangement is due to excessive sexual intercourse. I myself did not notice any signs of insanity until last February, but I distinctly remember a medical friend of mine, to whom I introduced him some eight or nine years ago, saying 'that man will fix in a madhouse'. I only laughed at this at the time, but still it made a great impression on my mind. If he really showed signs of insanity eight or nine years ago, it is clear the syphilis can have nothing to do with it. I shall be very happy to answer any further questions you may wish to ask me.'

On admission he happily listed what he called his 'deeds': that he was the Head of the Whole State and had an appointment with the Prime Minister, Lord Salisbury, that afternoon; that he had been selected as a prophet and was the most powerful man in the world; that he was the finest player of every kind of game and walked 200 miles every morning to get an appetite for breakfast. He could run a mile in five seconds and knew everything there was to know by inspiration. When asked what he thought of his surroundings he replied that he 'never saw such a damned lot of idiots in one place' in his life.

He settled happily on his ward but on 20 December was still full of grandiose plans and told the staff that he had grown four inches in height since admission and believed that his wife was growing too. On 25 January 1887 there is a note that he was not allowed to go to a Hospital dance because of his eroticism. He told the staff that his charms made all the ladies at the last dance comatose.

On 27 January a marked change in his behaviour was noted. He now stood alone on the ward talking to imaginary people and became less aware of his surroundings. Because he had bruised his hand he was moved to MIA ward on 2 July where he continued to decline. Apparently unaware of the staff and other patients he would walk around naked and was now dragging his left leg when he walked and slurring his speech.

On 3 November he was still confused and claiming to be Colonel Urquhart and that he had fought at Balaclava. Over the following months he continued to decline physically and mentally and on 6 August 1888 it was noted that he now had difficulty recognising Dr Hyslop, the assistant medical officer, thinking that he was a former resident of the Hospital but being unable to name him. In June 1889 he had the first of a series of convulsions which carried on uncontrolled for the rest of his time in the Hospital. He deteriorated to the point where he was described as 'living a purely vegetative life', and would repeat the words 'it's over' to himself or would rub his head violently and crunch his teeth as if in great pain or distress. By May 1890 it was clear that he was in the terminal stage of neurosyphilis. He became very weak and his convulsions stopped. On 23 May his wife visited and stayed at his bedside overnight. He died at two minutes to six on the morning of 24 May.

## 'He began to simulate a fit, but stopped when threatened with a cold bath'

Taken on 1 February 1888.

**William Budd, a 57-year old commercial traveller from Huntingdon, was admitted on 23 March 1887. He had previously been an inpatient at Bethlem from 10 February 1885 to 29 December 1886.**

*Has the delusion that he is possessed of boundless wealth, also that he is a great author and poet. Wanders about in an erratic manner and is very loquacious differing thus from his natural manner. I believe he has been under restraint on a previous occasion. His friends inform me that he has been sleepless for some time.*

Dr Donald MacRitchie, High Street, Huntingdon

*Has delusions that he is a great author and that he is related to certain of the nobility, which is not true. That he is only 20 years of age. Has been in an asylum before.*

Dr John Brooke Ridley, Huntingdon

His earlier admission had been for depression. At this time he had expressed thoughts that detectives were after him because he was responsible for the Egyptian war. The first symptoms of the present episode were that he arrived at his sister's house in London in a state of great excitement, announcing that he was going to ride a horse for Lord Sandwich and was going to write a book, for which he would be paid millions. He had continued to behave in an excited and strange manner for the next fortnight, was eccentric and extravagant in his dress and was reported to have bought bonnets for prostitutes in Regent Street. On admission his appearance was normal apart from the presence of a brightly coloured silk handkerchief stuck inside his waistcoat, and his pipe which he had stuck through a buttonhole of his coat. He continued to express his beliefs that he was 'the greatest political speaker or writer who has ever lived', and that he had been asked to stand for Huntingdon at the next election as well as enjoying close friendship with Lord Sandwich. This last claim was described as 'improbable' by the admitting physician. Mr Budd admitted that he must have been 'off his head' to have carried out some of his activities prior to admission, in particular taking fourteen prostitutes to a bonnet shop to get bonnets when his income was only thirty pounds a year.

In the days following admission he remained exuberant and elated. He stole from other patients and boasted that he could 'steal anything from a three-penny bit to a bloody elephant'. On 10 April 1887 he showed a letter to Dr Smith which he claimed had been sent from his family begging him to come home to them. The handwriting in the letter was strikingly similar to his own. He was unable to produce the envelope that it had arrived in and his application to be discharged home was refused. On 15 May he was reported to have tearfully informed a visiting clergyman that his eldest daughter was dying of consumption and asked if the clergyman could intercede with the doctors to allow him to go out and see her for the last time. When later questioned about this, he told the staff that it had been 'all a lie'. He was reported to have been upsetting female patients during Hospital chapel services (one of only a few events, other than the monthly patients' ball, which male and female patients attended at the same time) by winking at them. By November he was described as having become depressed by still being in hospital and was beginning to be abusive to staff members. On 5 November he was found lying naked on his back in his room, having emptied his chamber pot on the floor. When the attendants came into his room he began to simulate a fit, but stopped when threatened with a cold bath. There was little further change in his condition and on 14 March 1888 he was discharged uncured to London County Council's Cane Hill Hospital. A short poem is included in his case notes:

Mr Budd's 'parting shot' to Dr Savage, Bethlem's Physician Superintendent.


Dear Doctor, when the trumpet sounds
And God proclaims the judgement day
You'll try I know to be at least
Some fifty miles or more away
'Twill be no use, no tree no bush
Will hide you from God's searching eye
With other Savages you'll have
To toddle up your luck to try
You'll go to heaven I believe
But not to galleries II or III
With fifth-rate angels you will be
In lower gallery in M.I.B.
You'll daily scrub the gallery floors
And cleanse your brother angels' sores
You'll smooth their wings and comb their tails
And empty too their slops in pails
In course of years some three or more
You may be raised to gallery IV.


But Mr Budd's real parting shot came in a final note of October 1888. Apparently he was very troublesome at Cane Hill and had to be transferred to London County Council's asylum at Banstead, Surrey. When he had heard that Dr Savage was leaving Bethlem he had announced that 'the great end of his life was accomplished and that he had got him turned out'.

## 'She feels like a mere animal having lost her soul'

Taken on 23 March 1888.

**Sarah Taylor, also known as Maria, a 57-year old doctor's widow from Regent's Park, was admitted on 20 May 1887.**

*She walked about the room in a state of great agitation saying that she had been charged with crimes for which she would have to go to prison, which I find to be a delusion. She feels like a mere animal having lost her soul. She would prefer death to this state. Her son, Mr Charles Louis Taylor, informs me that she labours under the delusion that people accuse her of having had a child by her own father. Also she thinks evidence has been collected in Ireland of her having committed a felony.*

Dr Daniel Hack Tuke, Lyndon Lodge, Hanwell, Middlesex

*The patient is in a state of great mental distress and is under the impression that some thirty or forty people are plotting against herself and her son and that the latter is in danger of being dragged off to prison. She refused to reveal the nature of the charges. Her son tells me that she is continually writing letters, sometimes three and four a day, to the same person, many utterly incoherent. All of these have reference to the same subject – the question of her son's legitimacy. She also thinks she is accused of being a Protestant in disguise.*

Dr Harrington Sainsbury, 63 Welbeck Street, London

Soon after admission, she told the staff that she believed that she was going to be imprisoned for life in the Hospital and that she would commit suicide rather than undergo this. On 3 June she made three attempts to strangle herself with a handkerchief and pieces of braid torn off her dress. She was moved to Ward II. On the morning of 13 June she swallowed a quantity of carbolic disinfecting powder which she had found in the laundry. She vomited and fainted. Further vomiting was encouraged with emetics and she improved physically but was confined to bed for the next three days. On 23 June she swallowed some paint which had been left by a workman. Once again she was given emetics. She was found to be concealing pins in her hair, and string in her mouth, in order to get them into her room at night. On 31 July she was considered safe enough to be 'allowed to go about without gloves'.

Mrs Taylor was evidently still concerned about accusations of incest. In August 1887 she wrote a lengthy defence: 'I wish it to be known that I (Mrs Leith Taylor) had a sister who bore the same name as myself, i.e. Maria. This gave rise to errors and misrepresentations.

My sister Maria Hay was twice married. Her first marriage took place in 1848 two months previous to mine with Dr Taylor. She married a Mr John Walker of Aberdeen, by whom she had one son, Thomas Walker. She became a widow and after some years married a Mr Thomas Foster, by whom she had two sons, Edward who died and William Hay, named after my deceased father who died in 1844. The marriages were of my sister and the births were of her children. Should anyone doubt the accuracy of these statements, they can apply to Mrs Finnister, 4 Linkfield, Musselburgh of Scotland and likewise to Mrs Yuille, 28 Queen Mary's Avenue, Crosshill, Glasgow, as these reliable parties were well acquainted with both my sister and myself and can testify to the truthfulness that I had a sister. She died three years ago and Mr David Mitchell, Advocate, Aberdeen, transacted her business for her, and likewise my own affairs are duly registered. He can also be relied upon. My reason for mentioning these facts is that I have been accused of a dreadful crime, all owing to people imagining that these marriages and births belonged to me and were not my sister's but mine with my father who died in 1844 and is interred in France. I deny this awful calumny which will cost me my life. Should anyone take the trouble to investigate into this matter they will find that I have stated correctly and that I am condemned innocently for a crime I have never committed. I may add my father's name was William Hay. I forgot to mention I had one son by my husband Dr Taylor who died a short time after our marriage. I used to travel with my father many years ago, but no unlawful conduct took place.'

On 30 September she slipped away from the attendant when the patients were being collected together to go out to the airing court. She ran up the stone staircase to the next floor and threw herself down the stairs. She sustained a laceration to the back of her head, laying open a piece of bone about the size of a two-shilling piece. On 21 December she was less depressed and had not made any further attempts to harm herself. Her mental state made no further improvement and she was discharged uncured and transferred to Camberwell House, a private lunatic house in South London, on 16 May 1888.

## 'Keep the animals well fed in the zoo'

Taken on 22 February 1888.

**Frank Mitchell, a 30-year old boot maker from Dover, was admitted on 8 July 1887. He had previously been an inpatient in Bethlem from 24 March to 25 May 1876.**

*He has a delusion that the devil is in his abdomen. That he died, went to heaven and returned again to this world and now he must go to hell. Is emotional and slightly destructive. Herbert Alfred Mitchell (the brother) said he attempted to get out of a window, denied he was his brother, but was some other 'old Mitchell'.*

Dr Dennis Sidney Downes, 55 Kentish Town Road, London

*He was making a great noise shouting 'wait until the cock crows' and many other such remarks. He appears to have destroyed a part of the window pane and had to be restrained by force at the time I saw him.*

Dr Holland Hodgson Wright, 2 Ospringe Road, St John's College Park

Following admission he was initially restless and preoccupied and had to be fed by tube. By 21 July he was described as improved although he still believed that he had no delusions and that he acted quite correctly given the circumstances he found himself in. On 27 July he heard the voice of God telling him to kill Dr Savage and said that he felt he must do his duty even if he should die for it himself. On 1 August, he was found to have entered into a conspiracy with two other patients, Bates and Urquhart, to overpower Wilson, one of the attendants in MIA, grab his ward keys and escape the hospital. When searched, Mitchell was found to have some pebbles on him which were to have been used to put in keyholes to prevent the three from being followed. On 6 August he was reported to have said that he was getting another of the attendants, called Mortimer, out of the power of the devil and that 'forty days ought to do it'.

Mitchell wrote a letter dated 11 August to someone he described as his 'master mason', the doctors and attendants of the Hospital as well as the Czar of Russia. Before turning to address the Czar, he wrote to Hospital staff 'I beg to offer you my deepest and most sincere thanks for what you have done and are doing, and "the way you are doing it" for me. No doubt you think that I have been hard on Dr Savage and Dr Sampson, but believe me it is all for your good and it will not be long before you see that. But you no doubt would like to know what I want. I want each and every individual to do whatever he or she likes, and to accomplish it with as little bloodshed as possible.' As a postscript, he added 'Keep the animals well fed in the zoo'.

On 16 August he was described as speaking in a mysterious way and announced 'you have not done as I told you and I will burn down the bloody Hospital'. Through the autumn he continued to express delusions and told the staff that Urquhart, one of the patients with whom he had conspired, was Aaron, and attendant Wilson was the devil, and that he could arrange to have the moon fixed permanently over Bethlem. (Was he thinking of himself as Joshua, and perhaps of Bates as Moses?) On 10 January 1888 he told staff that he was managing everything in the Hospital and was working through Dr Savage. He made a great improvement in the spring, and on 13 March is described as being much less aggressive and troublesome. He was transferred to Witley. He returned to the Hospital improved and was discharged well on 25 April 1888.

## 'His manner at the dances is decidedly amorous'

Taken on 14 March 1888.

**Charles Kirk, a 25-year old barman from the Old Kent Road, was admitted on 17 August 1887.**

*On asking him what he complained of, he said he was afraid he should not grow up and also that he had a knife in his throat and that a cannon ball was about to explode in his throat, and altogether was strange and incoherent in his manner and expression. His step-mother, Elizabeth Kirk, says he has an unusual expression of face. He told her that detectives were after him. She tells me that he refuses to eat his meals and regards his food with suspicion as if he thought it was poisoned. His brother Charles said that he begged him to save him as someone was trying to shoot him.*

Dr Daniel Hooper, 9 Trinity Square, Southwark

*His aspect is one of great mental depression. He says that everyone is against him and that he wishes himself dead. He also told me that someone, he could not say whom, had attempted to poison him. His step-mother informs me that he says he wants to go somewhere for someone to shoot him as he wished to die. That he sits about in a melancholy manner refusing his food. His brother tells me that this morning he went out and said he wanted to go over the way and get shot as he wished to die away from home.*

Dr Thomas Evans, 3 Trinity Square, Southwark

His diagnosis on admission was alcoholic melancholia. No mention was made on either certificate of suicidal tendencies or family history of mental disturbance, but in a letter dated 17 August, Dr Hooper wrote: 'This patient has made at least two attempts to destroy himself, once by hanging, and I thought you ought to be made aware of this suicidal proclivity, which I omitted from the "form" for special reasons urged by the step-mother. Also the very important fact of heredity (the mother and a brother were insane). His present mother is his step-mother only ... The step-mother begged me not to put down on the "form" the suicidal tendency and the hereditary taint, but I hope I have not done wrong in giving you these facts by letter.'

About two years prior to admission Kirk had been diagnosed as having syphilis, from which he had recovered six months ago. Shortly after recovering he had begun to get depressed and in July 1887 had been noticed to be behaving strangely. He would sit at his meals and look at the food on the plate but not eat it. He would watch out through the door of his bar for hours, convinced that detectives were coming for him. He had wandered away from home and had taken to sitting in the cellar or coach house alone at night.

On 23 August 1887, six days after his admission to Bethlem, he was found to have twisted his bed sheet into a rope and told the attendants he had been trying to find how much weight it could bear. The staff suspected he was contemplating suicide but he denied this saying that he had no energy to do anything. By 3 October he is much brighter and on 25 October there is a note that he has been helped by having shower-baths. He is more lively and answering questions better but still not occupying himself in any way. On 10 February 1888 he was 'still inclined to sit in a chair all day' but his depression seemed much better and he was no longer considered at risk of suicide. He was transferred to Witley on 27 February.

On 22 May 1888 he returned from Witley, having put on weight. He no longer seemed depressed, but appeared to have no desire to go out of the Hospital or return to his occupation. His improvement was not maintained, and on 2 August there is a note that, for the past fortnight, he had refused food and had had to be fed twice a day by nasal tube. He told the attendants that he believed that syphilis was being put into his food. By 8 October he was taking food but remained miserable and depressed and was continually saying 'whatever shall I do?'. By 12 November he had improved again and on 9 January 1889 was described as more cheerful and dancing energetically although 'his manner at the dances is decidedly amorous'. By 30 March things were not so good and he was described as 'quiet and bleak-minded with a suspicious manner'. In June he complained that he could hear screams at night coming from one of the houses overlooking the airing court. He believed that murders were being carried out in the Hospital and said that he had seen people being laid out on a bed to be killed. On 15 June it was noted that he was sometimes impulsively violent and that he had been secluded for two days at his own request because of this. On 4 December he was described as still sullen, depressed and hearing voices. He was discharged uncured on 11 December, and taken home by his friends.

## 'He always has rather a satirical smile with a jaunty air'

Taken on 23 March 1888.

**Frederick George, a 19-year old student from Hackney, was admitted on 27 August 1887.**

*He is easily excited and laughs immoderately at trifles. He says the flies on his window make him sleepy. He says that if he passes a church he knows what the people within are doing as it comes through the walls to him. Charles Randall informs me that he has noticed the strange appearance of Frederick George and thinks the said George is frightened of him as he always stops singing and shouting when he hears Randall's footsteps.*

Dr James Pirie Martin, Box, Wiltshire

*He imagines he has had congestion of the brain and that there is now matter in the head. He thinks he hears voices out of trees which tempt him to do wrong. His memory is impaired, expression vacant and conversation rambling. Elizabeth Greenway informs me that Frederick George raves and laughs to himself when alone and paces the house thinking and saying 'the French are coming'.*

Dr John Ireland Bowes, Medical Superintendent, Wiltshire County Lunatic Asylum, Devizes, Wiltshire

Eighteen months prior to admission Frederick George had suddenly jumped off London Bridge and, having been rescued from the river, was sent to the country by his family for ten months. He was then sent to work on a dairy farm for three months but ran away to Weston Super Mare where he found work as an errand boy. He became 'odd and nonsensical in his talk' and was sent to live with Dr Martin, at Box in Wiltshire, for six weeks. While with Dr Martin he talked about animal magnetism and claimed to be able to read people's thoughts and complained that he was subject to impulses that he could not resist.

As well as providing a medical certificate for the admission of Frederick George to Bethlem, Dr Martin also sent a letter which can have left the Hospital in no doubt as to his view of the patient. 'You will soon see the sort he is – very conceited and full of delusions as to his own powers of knowing other people's thoughts, etc.', he wrote on 17 August, 'but I may tell you, in addition to what is in the certificates, that he often talks about what would happen if he were to kill anyone, and has frequently told me that when near animals he has felt impelled to kill them. I have not considered him dangerous or suicidal, but whether he will become so when he realizes that he is in an asylum is open to doubt. I fancy he masturbates but have not been able to make sure ... If you have leisure at any time, I should be glad to know whether you arrive at the same conclusion that I have reached, viz. that he is a hopeless case.'

On admission George claimed that he suffered constantly from headaches and felt that his brain had become desiccated. He claimed to have the ability to tell the characteristics of any person at a glance and could tell instantly if a murderer or other bad person came near to him. He claimed that he was very keen to find work to occupy himself, but when offered work in the Hospital garden he declined this.

On 20 September he was described as idle and unsociable and on 9 October as 'generally suspicious of everyone'. He remained much the same. On 21 December the notes say that he 'always has rather a satirical smile with a jaunty air'. On 8 March 1888 he told the attendant that there was a man on the roof of the Hospital who was talking to him and on 1 June he was observed to often appear to be listening to voices. He worked in the Hospital garden but showed no spontaneity in his manner or actions. On 29 August he was discharged uncured.

## 'Hardly bad enough to go to Bethlem Hospital again'

Taken on 2 March 1888.

**Frederick Brett, a 51-year old commercial traveller from Farnham, Surrey, was admitted on 12 October 1887.**

*He told me he was a rich man and should give up travelling. He was the best athlete. No man could swim like Sir Frederick Brett. He had sent £10 to Mr Sidebotham and £10 to Canon Hoste for charity. By James Brett, he had bought a brewery at Brading and had sold 400 barrels of beer on the way home. He had sold 20 packets of hops for me at £6-10 per hundredweight, which is not a fact.*

Dr Samuel George Sloman, 39 West Street, Farnham, Surrey

*Looks excited and talks incessantly. Thinks he is going to be a Member of Parliament and save the country from ruin. He had bought a big brewery which is not a fact. James Brett, brother, says that he is constantly drawing cheques and sending them all over the country. Says that he was a pupil of Tom Sayers and in the next breath that he was twenty-five years of age.*

Dr John Archibald Lorimer, 33 Castle Street, Farnham, Surrey

On admission he was elated, challenging anyone in the Hospital to a running race over five miles or to a boxing match. He told the staff that he was going to a pheasant shoot the next day and promised 20 brace of birds to the Hospital. On 17 November he was reported to have been very agitated on leaving the Chapel and told the attendant that his 'little woman', as he termed a female friend that he intended to marry, was breaking her heart over him and their forced separation.

On 14 February 1888 he was much more manageable and had become quieter. He was transferred to Witley. On 1 June he had returned to Bethlem and remained quiet although he was reported to have written a letter to his brother, James, in which he had said that he was going to die and wished to spend the end of his life at home. On 13 June he was given three weeks leave of absence and was discharged relieved on 4 July.

Frederick's recovery appears not to have been sustained. At the end of the year he suffered a paralytic fit, and his brother James was attempting to obtain the services of a male attendant to look after him at home. On 4 May 1889 James Brett wrote to Dr Savage: 'I beg to solicit your kind advice. My brother's indisposition necessitates much care and attention for his safety. He is quite harmless, being quiet, but unconscious of, and not at all responsible for, his actions – and yet he is hardly bad enough to go to Bethlem Hospital again.

Could you kindly grant an order for him to be at Witley. He seemed so well when he was there before ... My brother could be quietly taken to Witley by myself. It would be safer for him to be there than wandering about here in danger.' This request could not be met, as there was no direct procedure for admission to Witley. Only patients resident at Bethlem Hospital were sent there, and in the event Frederick Brett did not return to Bethlem.

## 'I received very great violence at the hands of the attendants in the B Ward'

Taken on 2 March 1888.

**John Clifford, a 42-year old gardener from Twickenham, was admitted on 4 February 1888.**

*Extremely violent to all around him. Sleeplessness. Delusions in regard to his family whom he accuses of wishing to poison him. I witnessed an onslaught made against his brother George Clifford. His brother said that he accused himself and others of having revolvers and intending to shoot him. Also that poison was put into his medicine and that he wanted to strangle him.*

Dr Samuel Lawrence Gill, Burlington Lodge, Whitton, Middlesex

*General restless mania, wild expression of face, incoherent talk. Told me his soul was lost. He is so violent that his arms have to be confined in a jean jacket. Mary Ann Clifford his wife told me he thinks all his friends are trying to poison him with strychnine (which is a delusion) and that he has tried to hit her and his own brother on several occasions.*

Dr William Montague Ball, Croxly House, Hounslow, Middlesex

Five years after his stay in Bethlem, John Clifford claimed, in a letter to Dr Smith, that the onset of his illness was due to what was known at the time as 'railway spine'.

'In November 1886 I was returning from Covent Garden by the 11am out from Waterloo in a dense fog. When the train had just got beyond the platform junctions, the train was stopped to shunt into another side platform to take two horse boxes. The engine of the previous train ran into us as we were stopping. I was thrown forwards then backwards, which wrenched my spine and afterwards brought on shock to the system. I was under treatment by Dr Lawrence Gill for five months, I began to get all right and gave him up. On 3 January 1888 I was at Kingston at a friendly party. I was taken just as if I should fall over dead, I had all my blood leave my extremities and flood my heart, had I lost my nerve nothing could save me. After about an hour when I was almost cowed, I got to Dr Shirtliff of Kingston. He examined me with his instrument and advised me on no account to undergo the exertion of getting home, but get back to my friend's place, and he would visit me in the morning. He also gave me a draught to take at once. I rallied after a rest and then would go home. I had Dr Lawrence Gill to me the next morning and was under him until I was taken on 4 February 1888 to Bethlehem.'

Following admission he was very restless and difficult to manage. On 7 February he tore up one of the panels in the padded room and bit the end off his gloves. He told the doctor that he could feel an invisible handkerchief around his neck that was strangling him and that he had seen Henry Lucca (a man the police were after) in his room at night. On 10 February he claimed that he was King John of England. On 18 February he was reported to be quiet for the first few hours of the morning. Then, after he had been up for about twelve hours, he began to lose self-control and became so violent that he had to be kept in bed and in the dark. By 10 March he was 'better and worse', having good days when he was quiet and easy to manage and then days when he was very violent, resisting anything that the staff wanted to do with him. On 18 March he was very noisy again and had to return to the padded room, but by May was more settled in his behaviour. On 20 May he was reported to be constantly walking around the grounds of the Hospital, doing several miles of walking each day. He was quiet and self-possessed and very deferential to staff. He acknowledged that he had been ill, but continued to complain that his brother had behaved very badly by him. On 6 June he was given leave of absence for one month and this was extended for a further month on 4 July. On 1 August he came up to the Hospital for review. All had been well apart from an episode when he had experienced a 'rush of blood to the head with a feeling of suffocation' which had left him helpless for six hours. He acknowledged that he had been excited when first admitted, but explained that this was an understandable reaction to having been ill treated at home. He was discharged well.

After his discharge, he kept up a (presumably) one-way correspondence with Dr Smith in order to complain about his treatment in MIB, writing, for instance, on 3 June 1889 that 'I was brought from a bed of sickness in a cruel and brutal manner by three cowardly blackguards; the ringleader was George Clifford, who is not a fit or proper person to enter any respectable house – his antecedents are well known at Richmond and Wandsworth Police Courts. I received very great violence (and bad language) at the hands of the attendants in the B Ward, especially Dimond, who is a cowardly brute and uses such bad language to the patients under his charge, how a committee of gentlemen can allow afflicted patients to be ill-used in the manner I have witnessed, on others as well as myself, is a mystery to me. There is only one attendant in the B Ward that did not ill-use the patients while I was an inmate of the B Ward. I shall ever remember the different treatment that is used towards the patients in No. IV Gallery by the attendants. There is no need for violence or bad language to be used to any patient, as there is always plenty of assistance to restrain a refractory patient.'

There is a final note, dated 28 July 1890, to say that he had been seen recently by the head attendant and seemed well although he still had animosity to the attendants in MIB.

# 'A gas explosion of a most alarming character'

Taken on 16 February 1888.

**Esther Dann, a 41-year old housewife from Lavender Hill, was admitted on 8 February 1888.**

*Incessant talking of a more or less disconnected character. Says that she has visions and knows that she has murdered her sister Elizabeth. Says that she is dying and that God will let her say but three things. States that she has three children. The patient has been under my care from the commencement of the attack. I have seen her constantly and observed its development from the simple excitement resulting from the shock caused by the accident.*

Dr Joseph Needham, 2 Westbury Gardens, Loats Road, Clapham Park

*Continual disconnected talking. Is under the impression that she sees visions and can work miracles. Her conversation rambles on visions and religion and other very absurd conversation. William Dann says that she asserts that she was thirty years younger than she actually was at the date of her marriage she being at that date thirty-two years of age. She also asserts that she is a prophetess and can predict. Elizabeth her sister says that she (Esther Dann) fancied herself Jesus and wished her to kneel as she had just performed a miracle.*

Dr Horace Osborne Bayfield, 123 Lavender Hill, London

The accident referred to in one of the certificates occurred in January 1888, and a local newspaper report gave the following account of it.

Terrific Explosion in Marmion Road

On Saturday morning last a gas explosion of a most alarming character took place at no. 12 Marmion Road, a house in the occupation of Mr and Mrs Dann ... About nine o'clock ... Mr and Mrs Dann were about to breakfast in the front room, which opens upon the back room by folding doors, when a boy employed in the house told his master that there was an escape of gas in the back room. He stated that the chandelier needed more water, and was instructed by Mr Dann to pour some water into it. The folding doors were shut, and the boy ... got a step-ladder and a jug of water to pour into the defective chandelier. Without the knowledge of the master he also appears to have brought a lighted candle, the room being darkened by the conservatory ... Standing on the step-ladder he proceeded to pour the water in, and in so doing brought the naked light of the candle into close proximity of the escape. A terrific explosion ensued. The boy was thrown to the ground, his hair and clothes catching on fire. A bundle of papers in a corner of the room was also caught alight, and the house would probably have been burnt down but for the prompt intervention of passers-by. Nearly every window in the house was blown out ... The boy rushed out of the front door, when some bystanders took him at once to Dr Bayfield's surgery, where he was attended to, and although very much shaken and scorched it was found that he had not received any permanent injury. Mrs Dann had a narrow escape from a heavy cornice pole falling on her in the front room ... The whole house has the appearance of having been wrecked, and both Mr and Mrs Dann and the servant were considerably shaken and alarmed. The house and contents were insured, and beyond the injuries to the boy (who is progressing favourably) no permanent damage has been done. Mr Dann possesses a unique collection of nearly 20,000 newspapers from every part of the world catalogued and bound in his library, and if the fire had reached them the loss would have been irreparable.'

On admission Mrs Dann's hair was noted to be very 'crisp and of a negro-like character' and to 'stand out very much all over her head' so that the physician wondered if she had an 'electrical condition'. She was incoherent and was apparently experiencing visual and auditory hallucinations and was placed in strong clothing in the padded room in FIB ward. On 14 February she was still very restless and incoherent and had been refusing food so that she had been fed by tube. There was little change in her condition over the following weeks and on 16 March it was noted that her feet had swollen from her constant standing about. She had to be tied in bed through April and remained in strong clothes during the day. By 10 October she had been sleeping in strong clothes every night for a fortnight, but without having her arms restrained. On every night during this period she had torn up her bedding, and so was forced to wear side arm dress in bed for the next twelve days or so. On 21 November she was discharged uncured.

On 28 November the discharge was rescinded and she was readmitted as a paying patient. She was given an extra sleeping draught, which seemed to improve her sleep at nights. She was discharged uncured to Hoxton House, a private lunatic house in East London, on 26 December.

## 'She tore up her bedding and clothes'

Taken on 16 April 1888.

Helen Smith, a 35-year old single woman from Peckham, was admitted on 22 February 1888. She had previously been an inpatient at Bethlem from 1 November 1881 to 21 February 1882, and was photographed by Francis Galton at some point during this earlier admission (see page 12).

*Sleeplessness, utter incoherence. Has taken intense aversion to her kindest friend. Is violently restless and destructive and has to be forcibly restrained from doing mischief.*
Dr Cameron Gillies, Walcot House, Brockley

*Constant incoherent talking. Violent unless restrained.*
Dr Francis Sydney Smyth, 284 Brockley Road, Brockley

On admission she was described as 'very noisy, incoherent and violent' and was confined in the padded room of FIB ward where she tore up her bedding and clothes. On 8 March she was still in the padded room and whenever tied up was violent and noisy but had begun to take food. On 9 March she had torn her fingernails by scraping the floor and had made her face bleed by picking at it. She was made to wear strong clothes and gloves. On 26 March she was a little quieter and was wearing ordinary clothes and no gloves for the first time. She improved very little and on 10 October was described as quiet and able to help out with ward work, but still without complete control over her actions. On 19 March 1889 she was transferred to Witley and returned to Bethlem on 30 April with reports that she had done very well. She was discharged well on 1 May.

# 'There are a large number of men here with very little the matter with them'

Taken on 24 March 1888.

**Daniel Benstead, a 30-year old master barman, who had been working in Canada, was admitted on 14 March 1888.**

*Incoherence of speech. Delusions, e.g. that he has a right to the Crown of England and that the Queen has abdicated and taken a villa for her own residence so that he may live at Windsor Castle. That he can hear people speaking in Canada from Surrey. By Clara Benstead, that he has written a letter to the Queen on the subject of her abdication. That he maintains that Clara Benstead has entered into a plot to shoot him.*

Dr Ernest Garstin Anderson Morshead, 12 Quarry Street, Guildford, Surrey

*That he believes he is the rightful heir to the English Crown. That the Queen has taken a villa previous to abdicating. Much incoherence and delusions in speaking and that the Queen and Prince of Wales consent to his being King. Chrissy Benstead states that he said she was going to shoot him. She also states that he has written to the Queen asking if she has abdicated or not. John Benstead states that he sent witches into his room to kill him.*

Dr Morney Coppin, Hazeldean, Farnborough, Hampshire

In October 1887 he had stopped work and had been observed to do nothing all day but sit and read the Bible and John Bunyan's *Pilgrim's Progress*. He had spent nearly all his money in Canada before his family persuaded him to return to England. On his return, he had the delusion that he had come home to England as heir to the throne and expected to be crowned. He had written twice to Queen Victoria.

On admission to the Hospital, he explained that he had had visions of Ministers of God who had told him that he was heir to the throne because he was 'of the blood of David'. These visions had also told him that the Prince of Wales was on his side. He believed that he was being followed and watched because of this. He considered his hospital confinement to be unjustified, and wrote a letter to the American consul in London on 27 March appealing for help, in which he maintained for good measure that 'there are a large number of men here with very little the matter with them – some a little mentally and physically weak – and I consider the British Authority at the top of the ladder are to blame greatly for it.' He slept and took food well, but his condition remained unchanged. On 14 August he had written to the President of the United States asking him to intercede on his behalf, and he addressed his father as 'His Majesty' in letters.

On 10 October it was recorded that he had suddenly broken a window in No. IV ward and had been moved to MIA. When asked about this, he had replied that his action was no more unreasonable than his detention in the Hospital. On 4 February 1889 he was described as unchanged and was still writing as much as ever and as full of delusions. He was discharged uncured on 13 March. On 26 May, Benstead wrote from America to the Hospital's Physician Superintendent concerning his treatment: 'I don't blame you for all the impious works carried on there, for I believe they get such as you there to do their dirty deeds, and you have to do it, or go, and perhaps if you had of been [sic] left to yourself, and me left alone, I would not of been in there long.' He spent the rest of the year in North America.

His ideas concerning the machinations of the British Royal Family, and his sense of grievance concerning his detention at Bethlem, continued at least until 1891, when he wrote to George Davis, the Hospital's head attendant, blaming Queen Victoria 'and the rest of the rebels in this country' for 'shutting me up exceeding a year and trying to make me a lunatic'. He signed this letter 'Your late patient, Daniel H. Benstead – a merciful son; not, like a host of Bethlem Hospital servants, unmerciful and doing the wicked work of an ungodly government.'

## 'From thinking about it too much, he told me he could not sleep'

Taken on 31 March 1888.

Samuel Stow, a 48-year old farmer from Kersey, Suffolk, was admitted from Ipswich Borough Asylum on 23 March 1888.

*From our observations and from answers to questions, depression of spirits, slowness of speech, not proper regard for his own wife, sad expression of countenance and alteration of manner. His brother, Joseph Stow, says he will shoot himself, has chosen a place to do it. Is continually moaning and says he can create a world.*

Dr Joseph Clement Norman, Hadleigh, Suffolk

*General haziness of things that have happened. His speech is thick and slowness of delivery. Incoherent ideas of what had happened recently. Defective memory. Said he had nothing to live for. James Matthew, Relieving Officer, Hadleigh, informs me that his gait, demeanour and character are much changed the last month. Is desponding and wishes to put an end to his life.*

Dr Stanley Stenton Hoyland, 10 Museum Street, Ipswich, Suffolk

In support of his admission, his brother Joseph wrote to the Hospital committee that governed admissions, on 26 March, 'with regard to the cause of the mental condition of my brother Samuel, I have no doubt in my own mind that it was from worrying so much about his business. He farmed two hundred acres of land, and till seven years ago had been successful; then unfavourable seasons and low prices came, still he struggled on, up till just before last Christmas. He used to see in the papers that distress was being put in for rent in many cases, and he thought, as his own rent was in arrears, that his turn would come next. Then from thinking about it too much, he told me he could not sleep. His smaller creditors agreed to take ten shillings in the pound, his bankers and two of his larger creditors carrying on the farm till next Michaelmas. And they were giving him twelve shillings per week to manage the farm, which he continued to do till Christmas last. So it has left him now with no income at all.' Joseph further explained to the committee that 'I would gladly help to pay something for him if I could. I did make an effort with a sister who lives with me to pay for him for six weeks at Ipswich. I have myself been unfortunate through the fall in the price of land.'

On admission Samuel Stow was in a state of partial stupor but was sleeping and eating fairly well. On 30 March he was reported to be standing about the ward or airing court on his own for most of the day, taking no interest in anything. On 14 April he had to be fed by tube and this was continued until 3 May when he suffered a collapse and was considered too weak to be tube-fed. However, in the evening he was fed in bed by tube. On 4 May he had developed symptoms of pneumonia with dullness to percussion at both lung bases. He was tube-fed again but appeared to be dying. He died at 7.40p.m. on 4 May. At post mortem his lungs were congested and heavy with evidence of bronchopneumonia at both bases.

# 'I did not imagine for one moment that I was about to be branded as a lunatic'

Taken on 31 March 1888.

**Arthur Postans, a 44-year old former pharmaceutical chemist of Baker Street, was admitted on 30 March 1888.**

*On Friday 23 March A.W. Postans came to the vestry of St David's Church and presented a written document drawn up in legal phraseology by himself which he requested the vicar, the Reverend J.S. Sinclair, to sign. Postans said he had been appointed Head of the Church of England and wished to hand over St David's to Sir Charles Warren because he was the Head of Law and Order and therefore wanted the vicar's signature to the document produced giving up his title to the building to A.W. Postans. Mrs Postans, the wife of the above, informs me that while living at 55 Baker Street he was always worrying the clergymen in the neighbourhood and called on Canon Leigh and his curate, Mr Barnard, as many as 40 times a day respecting the Tyndale Memorial until warned off by the Police. Also that he attended the daily services at Quebec Chapel in the neighbourhood of Soho and used every day to call and enquire of the Chapel Keeper what time the service commenced and always took with him to the service a bag containing two large family bibles weighing upwards of 20 lbs, papers connected with the Tyndale Memorial and a large picture more than one yard long in the shape of a scroll.*

Dr Hugh Webb, Ingleville, Parsons Green, Fulham

*Incoherence, rambling and not connected at all in conversation. Has delusions that he has a mission from God and the Roman Catholics to hand over St David's Church to the Roman Catholics. Fancies that the clergymen at St David's have conspired together to rob him of his business and that they have sent in the doctors to make him a scapegoat. Said that I represented the money part of the transaction. From Mrs Postans, that he has been for some time very lost and wandering generally in his ideas. Worrying the clergymen at Quebec Chapel.*

Dr James Robert Hill, Peterborough House, Fulham

On 3 April, Postans addressed a long and rambling explanation of his actions to Dr Webb, whom he considered to have had him admitted to Bethlem under false pretences: 'When you called upon me at my dear wife's house, 32 Bottridge Road, Fulham, SW, on Good Friday last and said Mr Sinclair desired you to go with me to the Ecclesiastical Commissioners respecting the document I gave him, in connection with his church on

Parsons Green, and which he thoroughly approved of at the time, I did not imagine for one moment that I was about to be branded as a lunatic – for honestly endeavouring to put right on behalf of St Mary's & Quebec Chapel Missionary Association and the William Tyndale Memorial Movement – a really sharp trick on the part of the clergy of the Established Church of England – without the intervention of the law.'

On 31 May there is a note that he thought that a Roman Catholic priest who had come to see another patient, was specifically sent to the Hospital with reference to the Tyndale Memorial Movement. On 6 June it was recorded that he believed that everything that happens to him, even a toothache, has some special hidden meaning relating to the Memorial. He walked past another patient, Walther Wolfram (see pages 18–19), greeted him as a 'Lutheran', and was surprised when Wolfram called him a blackguard. On 8 August he was moved to No. IV Gallery where he did not quarrel or interfere as much with other patients as he had done in No. III. On 12 February 1889 he was moved to MIA ward because he had been increasingly noisy and abusive. He was discharged uncured on 27 March. There is a final note, dated July 1889, to say that he had been seen at Peckham House, a private lunatic house in South London, where he was now 'filthy in ideas and language' but his other symptoms were as before.

## 'I have been very ill, but am better, thank God'

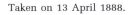

Taken on 13 April 1888.

**Eleanor Herbert, a 41-year old gentlewoman from Richmond, was admitted on 6 April 1888.**

*I have treated her for melancholia since June 1887. She has during that period been under the delusion that her soul is lost. She has a decided aversion to consulting a clergyman on the subject. At my next interview with her that delusion was if possible stronger than before. The results of conversation with her are very unsatisfactory. She sleeps badly. Her appetite is good. She has become very slovenly in her habits. Her father, Mr James Lynch, informs me that she is at times very violent, rushes out of the house suddenly and wanders about the streets for hours. She was away for three days in February 1888 and was found by the Police at Chiswick. In the present month she went into several shops in the neighbourhood and took up trifling articles of no use whatsoever to her. She was detected in one (Whiteley's).*

Dr Michael Henry Taylor, 32 Church Road, Richmond, Surrey

*Stolid aspect, incoherence, incapacity to realise what is said and evident effort to appear calm and reasonable. No effort to keep herself clean and tidy. Melancholy. Her father states that she cannot be unwatched for more than a moment. Otherwise she breaks out, even from the windows, steals his keys and other objects and is violent when restrained.*

Dr John Sarsfield Comyn, 32 Dawson Place, London

On admission she was 'very wet and dirty' and had destroyed her clothing and was sent to FIA ward. On 9 April she was reported to be noisy at night and still very dirty and destructive, requiring the use of strong clothing. Later in the month she wrote to her father, apparently under the mistaken impression that she was about to be discharged: 'I shall see you today, as I am going home. Did May bring little George? I have adopted him as my child, he is a dear little fellow ... I am going to Bristol today to bring Hal home. I want him to come home. I have been very ill, but am better, thank God.'

On 30 April there is a note that for the past week she has been in the continuous bath every other day, increasing by an hour each day. On 21 June she is described as unchanged. She is having the baths every other day, alternating with dry pack. She is still 'filthy and destructive', but is reported to have said that she is 'perfectly happy and has never been in such a jolly place'. On 27 June she was discharged uncured to London County Council's Cane Hill Hospital. There is a final note dated 10 October containing news from Cane Hill that she is 'getting better'.

## 'I must at times have been a source of anxiety to you all'

Taken sometime in 1890.

**Thomas Skinner, a 41-year old grocer from Spalding, Lincolnshire, was admitted on 22 March 1890.**

*He declared he had committed 'millions' of sins and great crimes for which he had to be punished and that his soul was lost without hope of forgiveness, that all his friends have forsaken him, and that he has ruined and disgraced all his family whereas such is not the case. His wife, Sarah Hannah Skinner, states that for some time past he has been unable to sleep, spending much of the night imagining that his business was ruined, dwelling upon minor matters until they appeared to him untoward difficulties, that his friends and relations had forsaken him and that he was the worst sinner on earth.*

Dr Henry Tournay Stiles, 18 The Terrace, London Road, Spalding, Lincolnshire

*He told me he had committed great sins and that the police were coming to arrest him. He said his soul was lost, that he had committed the* unpardonable sin against the Holy Ghost and said that he often felt impulses to take away his own life but was too cowardly to act on them. His wife told me that her husband had been depressed for two years, that his memory had lately failed, so that his accounts were inaccurately kept. That he was suspicious of everyone and under the impression that there was a conspiracy against him. Also that he was under many delusions.

Dr Andrew Mercer Adam, The Church Close, Boston, Lincolnshire

His initial admission diagnosis was general paralysis with melancholic onset and the prognosis was given as bad, but this was crossed out at a later date and the revised diagnosis of post-influenzal melancholia inserted, possibly due to a letter written to Dr Smith from his wife on 29 March, advising that Thomas had 'had an attack of this influenza epidemic just before his mental trouble came on'.

Following admission he remained very depressed and distracted by auditory hallucinations. On 29 March he was asked to sign his name and wrote only the word 'Petrolium'. When it was suggested to him that his name was Skinner, he wrote that down instead but was unable to recall his Christian names. On 5 April he refused his food and had to be fed by tube. He was transferred to MIB ward. On 21 April when approached by a medical officer he began to moan in a dramatic and subdued voice 'Doctors again' and 'I am the wrong man'. On 25 June he is said to be much quieter and more rational. On 22 July he was much brighter but still expressing doubts as to whether he has done wrong and that people will have to suffer for him. He was sent to Witley and returned apparently well on 19 August. He was then granted three weeks leave and, when this was successful, was discharged well on 10 September.

On 10 January 1891, Skinner wrote to Dr Smith from Manchester, where he had been staying for a few days on his way home from a fortnight or so of rest and recuperation in Scotland and the Lake District: 'I suffer much in my head, cannot read but little and am soon knocked up, my left leg at times fails me if at all worried. I often think of you and the company of doctors, how kind you must have been with me in every affliction. I often trouble myself about you all, I must at times have been a source of anxiety to you all. For twenty-five years I have worked very hard and lived for others, and have stood by the beds of every kind of suffering known by doctors, clergy, ministers, nurses, etc. Mrs Skinner and myself have truly lived for others and have had the richest comfort in it all until this affliction came some weeks before I was sent to you. I suffered much strong constipation and well remember I had a peculiar shock from my head to my left foot in the WC, the effects I feel unto this day, though am much better in my general health but not equal to a whole day's business.

Your kind letter at Christmas cheered me, though I hoped you would not find me out. I sincerely pray you and all to forgive me for my mysterious conduct, for weeks I knew not what I was doing and yet I must confess I knew at times. Let me assure you, all that know me now and before, that I have been moral and tried to serve God in the station of life that I am in, helping the helpless and was always bright and cheerful. My kind regards to Cantell Senior.

I fear I am imposing on your time, for I know your busy life, but I feel it my duty to write to you. Any advice you feel inclined to give me to prevent further trouble I shall be most thankful for, thanking you most sincerely, also Drs Hyslop, Corner and company.'

## 'Now entirely restored to health, and seeking an appointment as governess'

Taken sometime in 1890 or 1891.

**Jessie Scott, a 31-year old single schoolmistress from Ealing, was admitted on 20 June 1890. She had previously been an inpatient at Bethlem from 20 April 1886 to 9 February 1887.**

*Is very depressed in spirits; has many delusions, hears voices which terrify her and order her to do different acts such as not to take food. Has lost her memory of things which occurred lately. Her sister, Miss Ada Scott, informs me that she had a previous attack three years since, that she has many delusions; viz, that voices call her dreadful names, that a sound of any kind gives to her the impression of words spoken, that she refused to take food this morning on account of the voices.*

Dr Robert Graves Burton, 1 Gloucester Villas, Hanwell, Middlesex

*From being bright, active and intelligent I find her looking gloomy, vacant and torpid. In conversation she is slow to answer and her memory of recent events is a blank. She says that she is being persecuted, that she hears voices at night who repeat that they have now proved her to be a prostitute, that they read her thoughts and repeat things. That her food (which she often refuses) gets hard and changes before it gets into her, all of which are delusions in my opinion. Her mother, Salomi Scott, says that she attaches undue significance to domestic articles such as the pepper box or her food before she eats it, that she is upset by the noise of the spoons, that people try to prove that she (Jessie Scott) is not her mother's child.*

Dr Herbert Arthur Smith, 19 Grange Road, Ealing

Her admission diagnosis was acute melancholia and her prognosis given as good. At admission her hallucinations were very troubling. Heard in both ears, the voices were usually distinct but sometimes harder to hear as if they came from a great distance. The voices used bad language and called her a prostitute. They echoed her thoughts and kept her awake at night. She could hear the voices most clearly in her right ear but those heard in her left ear were less distinct and heard with an 'indescribable confused feeling'.

On 7 July her hallucinations and delusions were described as being as distinct as before. On 19 December she is noted to be occupying herself quietly with sewing, but still troubled by voices. She remained unchanged and was discharged uncured on 10 June 1891. By the spring of 1892, she had recovered sufficiently to be actively seeking employment, and wrote to the Hospital on 25 April: 'Nearly eleven months ago, I was discharged from Bethlehem Hospital as uncured: being now entirely restored to health, and seeking an appointment as governess, I am in correspondence with several ladies ... Previous to making final arrangements to teach anyone's children, it is imperative that I should have a certificate of mental health. May I ask you to give me one?' But Jessie Scott was re-admitted to Bethlem on 30 July 1895, and was discharged uncured for a second time on 31 July 1896.

## 'Asked where she was, she replied "in Hell"'

Date of photograph unknown.

**Florence Wakeley, a 20-year old single woman from Rainham in Kent, was admitted on 22 October 1890.**

*She has general incoherence of manner and delusions of sound in saying that she heard voices. Violence to sister told to me by her mother, Mrs R.U. Wakeley. Throwing herself on the ground in the street saying she is lost told to me by her nurse, Miss Stevenson.*

Dr Henry Penfold, Rainham, Sittingbourne, Kent

*The patient is obviously extremely miserable, unable to converse or take in the meaning of questions but is inclined to stare vacantly, playing the while with the questioner's hand. She tells me that voices tell her how wicked she is, that her soul is lost and that Jesus is coming for her. Thomas Stanley Wakeley (patient's father) tells me that she has been getting very miserable lately, has thought that she is being watched and that she hears voices in the air.*

Dr Herbert Pennell Hawkins, St Thomas' Hospital, Albert Embankment, London

Her diagnosis on admission was melancholia (stupor) and the prognosis described as 'tendency to chronic instability or dementia but may recover from this'. In her past history, she had two earlier episodes of depression. About twelve months prior to admission she had become convinced that Jack the Ripper was after her with a knife, but this had only lasted for a few days. In February 1889, she had been ill for about three months during which time she had been convinced that people were after her and had shown violence to her family. She appeared to have made a complete recovery from this until the current episode.

On admission she was described as being slow in answering questions and staring ahead as if in some state of ecstasy. When asked where she was, she replied 'in Hell' and identified one of the attendants as a 'devil' and the assistant medical officer as 'Jesus'. She became very agitated and frightened at the sight of a stethoscope and would not allow the doctor to examine her with it.

On 29 October she was still in a stupor but was taking food well. On 2 November she was seen to be rubbing her eye with her fingers and told one of the attendants that she had been told that she must take it out. As a consequence of this she was made to wear gloves in bed at night. On 5 November she took the parrot out of its cage and wrung its neck but was unable to explain why she had done this and on 1 December it was recorded that she tried to kiss one of the clinical assistants. By the end of December she seemed to be recovering. On 28 December she was slightly more communicative and on 3 February 1891 she was transferred to Witley. She returned well to the Hospital on 17 March and was then allowed home on leave before being discharged well on 22 July. Subsequent to this, Florence Wakeley was re-admitted as a patient six times, spending a total of seven years at Bethlem between May 1892 and May 1902. On each occasion she was discharged relieved or recovered.

## 'If you don't discharge me by tomorrow I shall issue a writ against you'

Probably taken in March 1892.

**John Bishop-Culpepper, a 45-year old solicitor from Clapham, was admitted on 29 July 1891. He had previously been an inpatient at Bethlem from 24 December 1887 to 10 April 1888.**

*Continually talking in an incoherent manner. Will not answer questions distinctly and calls out very loudly.*

Dr Corrie Jackson, 5 Great Marlborough Street, London

*That he was unaware of his present position and surroundings. That his conversation was wandering and absurd and his general aspect that of dementia.*

Dr Charles John Ogle, 1 Cavendish Place, Cavendish Square, London

His admission diagnosis was given as acute mania in general paralysis and his prognosis was described as doubtful. On admission he was extremely excited and noisy, shouting at the top of his voice. He spoke in rhyme and was making everyone around him kings. He was incontinent in his bed. He was treated with increasing doses of hyoscine and this helped him to sleep at night, although he was still very noisy. By 4 November he had settled and was sleeping six hours each night and was able to settle to read a newspaper. He seems to have maintained some degree of this improvement, but in the spring of 1892 began to threaten to sue the Hospital for illegal detention. On 23 May, for example, he wrote to Dr Smith 'I have been detained here by you forty-three weeks without the slightest occasion for it. If you don't discharge me by tomorrow I shall issue a writ against you personally for £1290'.

The Hospital made no arrangements for his early discharge, but it did allow him three weeks leave starting on 22 June. A day after his leave had started, Bishop-Culpepper returned with a letter for a fellow patient, William Chalk (see pages 62–64), stating that he (Bishop-Culpepper) had taken out a summons at the Mansion House against Chalk for an assault, and that Chalk would have to defend himself in open court. It turned out that the alleged assault had never taken place, but the pair had devised this scheme as a means by which Mr Chalk might publicly demonstrate his sanity. Bishop-Culpepper had also visited Mr Chalk's brother while on leave, and claimed to have instructions from Mr Chalk to bring an action against the Hospital for illegal detention. He had pawned his waist-coat, and Hospital staff found several other pawn tickets on him. His three weeks' leave was promptly cancelled, and he was detained at the Hospital.

On 12 July he was allowed out for the afternoon with a woman he claimed (but Hospital staff doubted) was his wife. He did not return to the Hospital that evening as agreed, but sent in a letter saying that he was going abroad for a fortnight and was going to give £100 to attendant Wilson. On 13 July he was found in the street near the Hospital and brought back in again. There was no further change in his condition and he was discharged uncured on 28 September.

## 'He could hear voices saying that he ate too much'

Probably taken in March 1892.

Jacob Troeschel, a 62-year old baker from Eastbourne,
was admitted on 23 September 1891.

*He was very slow in answering questions, which was not his usual habit. He was very sad and melancholy because he heard voices talking that he could not understand. He thought people were following him to take him away. Said he was in trouble because he had been indecent and had lost his wife's money. Before I left the house he went out of the room and took off his clothes in the passage. His wife, Mrs Catherine Troeschel, says that fourteen days ago he wanted to make a speech to an imaginary audience out of the bedroom window. Four days ago he took off his clothes on the landing and wanted to go through the town to show himself off.*

Dr Henry Habgood, Stafford House, Upperton Road, Eastbourne, Sussex

*Sitting in one place without paying attention to surrounding objects. Sullen in manner and delays answering questions. His wife has told me that he has several times taken off his clothes in the passage outside the bedroom. Gets up and walks about room most of the night. Thinks people are waiting outside to remove him or hear him make a speech.*

Dr John Agar Matson, 8 Seaside Terrace, Eastbourne, Sussex

His admission diagnosis was melancholia and his prognosis given as fair. At the time of admission he complained that other people looked at and talked about him; he could hear voices saying that he ate too much and was 'a great lump of pudding'. At home he had heard his neighbours talking about him, but in the Hospital it was the voices of strangers that he couldn't recognise. On 20 October he was described as 'dull and morose' and on 4 December as 'still very depressed'. Things gradually improved so that on 29 March 1892 he went to Witley. He returned to Bethlem on 26 April and the next day was discharged well.

## 'It was thought he was so much better lately'

Probably taken in March or April 1892.

**John Wicks, a 60-year old farmer from Wiltshire, was admitted on 28 December 1891.**

*He complains of constant pains in the head, unable to remember or do anything. Life was not worth living for, says everything is wrong and that he is not worth anything also that he gave his knife to his niece for fear he should do anything wrong to himself. Elizabeth Mary Wicks, his niece, says that after the accident on 14 February he saw an angel who distributed crowns and asked to have his knife taken away as he could not trust himself.*

Dr Thomas Fitzherbert Snow, The Hermitage, Box, Wiltshire

*Is restless, appears depressed in mind, complains of constant pain in head, says that life is a worry to him and different from what it used to be and that he is tempted to do away with himself. Mary Ann Wicks (wife), that he proposed to her that they should both throw themselves into water. Large inordinate appetite. Has delusions that everything is filthy and dirty in the house.*

Dr Arthur George Wood, Corsham, Wiltshire

He was thought to have become nervous after an accident in February 1891 during which his back and spine had been bruised but he had not sustained a head injury. He had sustained financial losses due to wet summers and had recently changed to another farm.

On admission he was more settled and told the doctor that he no longer believed he was ruined but still complained of headaches and that he was unable to apply himself to anything. His mood fluctuated and on 30 December he was more agitated and restlessly paced around the Hospital. He told anyone he met that he was ruined 'monetarily and morally'. By 2 January 1892 he had improved again, and asked if he could visit his farm to do some odd jobs. He told the attendants that he felt that he was robbing the Hospital because he wasn't paying for his food. By 30 January he was described as 'bright and cheerful'. He realised that his previous ideas had been 'wrong through wrong imaginations' and told the doctor he now regarded his prospects in farming as fair. On 2 February he was sent to Witley to convalesce and on 16 March was granted one month leave of absence to go home. Three times this was extended by another month, on 13 April, 11

May and 8 June respectively, upon the recommendation of Dr Snow, one of the original certifying doctors. On 17 June, the wife of Mr Wicks wrote to the Hospital with tragic news. 'I am deeply grieved to have to tell you of my dear husband's death. It was thought he was so much better lately, as he attended church on Sunday and a club dinner on Monday, and he daily attended to the business. On Saturday morning he went to see one of his men who works in the field and he thought him better, but I am sorry to tell you shortly after he was found dead in the brook.' An inquest found that he had drowned.

# 'She asked if she could be buried in the Hospital garden'

Taken in the Hospital's airing court sometime in 1892.

**Ellen Hamilton, a 41-year old single woman from St John's Wood, was admitted on 10 January 1892.**

*Is constantly complaining of people intentionally annoying her by telephoning into her ears, by attempting to pull out her hair and by generally annoying her. Her servant resident in the house (Amelia Kerr) has called my attention to the fact that she attempted to commit suicide by drowning in the adjoining canal on 1 January 1892 and the state of her wearing apparel satisfied me that she had been quite immersed in water.*

Dr William Sedgwick, 101 Gloucester Place, Portman Square, London

*While I was talking to her she kept her clothes held up to her knees and appeared afraid to drop them, at one moment saying the floor was wet, at another that there was an escape of gas. She told me that people had extorted money from her by means of the telephone, that her house had been blown up and that the whole place was full of water. Susan Glyn, sister of above, of Turnchapel near Plymouth, Devon told me that her sister sometimes walked about all night, that she accused people of stealing her property, that she heard voices through imaginary telephones and that she had attempted to drown herself.*

Dr Horace George Turney, St Thomas' Hospital, Albert Embankment, London

Her history was that over the previous five months she had told friends and family that she believed that her house was going to be blown up by a gas explosion and that people were going to pour oil over her. Friends had noticed that she always seemed to be acting as though someone was talking to her and telling her to do things. Following admission she would sit for most of the day in a chair and would resist any attempts by the staff to move her. For example, it took the efforts of three attendants to put her to bed. She continued to complain about people telephoning into her ears in order to make unpleasant accusations and to repeat her thoughts. These people she said had destroyed her house and had murdered her on six occasions.

On 16 January she was described as still keeping quiet when left alone, but resisting being taken to dinner and to bed. It was still taking three attendants to dress and undress her. On 4 February she had made some improvement and, although she had not lost her ideas about the house being destroyed, she was no longer hearing the telephone voices. On 29

April she asked if she could be buried in the Hospital garden and this appears to have been a symptom of worsening depression. She was very miserable and began to shout at night, was moved to FIB ward where she had to wear strong clothing. On 4 October she was in a state of 'confusion and melancholic agitation'. On 10 December the notes indicate that she has depressive delusions and is saying that she is dead and has 'no lungs, no heart, no body'. She told the doctor that her brain had been cut out and that she had seen it lying about on the floor of the Hospital. By 6 April 1893 she was having treatment with prolonged baths and had become very noisy and excited. She was still claiming that she was dead and that all her organs had been removed. On 19 April she was discharged uncured and admitted to Camberwell House, a private lunatic house in South London.

## 'Only he can reform the Lunacy Act'

Probably taken in July 1892.

**William Chalk, a 39-year old civil engineer from New Barnet, was admitted on 1 February 1892.**

*He informs me that he has just brought out several patents all of which are going to turn out well and that he expects to make good things out of them. That he has offered two of them to the War Office and from the way they have been received there is not the slightest doubt they will be great successes. When I saw him he could not leave the house because he had not a penny in his pocket to pay the cabman in whose cab he had been driving about all day, or to pay the waiter of the restaurant at which he had lunched, both of whom were waiting at his door to be paid. He was excited and talked at great length of the magnificence of his patents, the description of their nature shewing that they are absurdly improbable. Thomas Cradock Chalk, brother of the patient, informs me that he is an undischarged bankrupt and for several days he has supposed that he is about to become possessed of considerable wealth and has accordingly left his wife at home and has been running up bills at hotels and shops without having any money to meet them. Has been driving in a hired carriage and pair, and also hires cabs and is unable to discharge the cabman the whole day because he has not a penny in his pocket.*

Dr James Samuel Risien Russell, 94 Wimpole Street, Cavendish Square, London

*He told me that he is about to make millions of money by means of a patent for protecting ships of war by armour plating. That such consists of two excessively thin layers of steel containing powdered cork and that this would cost about one-quarter of the present price of armour plating. Tells me that he went about all yesterday in cabs although having no money and did not think it unreasonable.*

Dr James McDonald Gill, 33 Trinity Square, Southwark

About five years earlier he had disappeared from home for a week. When he returned home he had said that he had got lost on the Underground after having a fainting attack. He could remember getting out at King's Cross but then had not known what he was doing until it had occurred to him to send his brother a telegram. In 1889 he had had an episode of illness very similar to the current one. He became excited and extravagant and had become bankrupt through this. He had subsequently been imprisoned for a year for passing a false cheque. About three weeks before his admission to Bethlem, he had taken his children to a pantomime although he had insufficient funds to afford it and had become progressively more and more extravagant. He left home and took rooms at the Hotel Metropole and then moved to the Savoy and then the Arundel running up huge bills at each of them. His admission diagnosis was given as delusional and his prognosis described as fair.

During his first days in Bethlem he was able to explain more to the doctors about his patents. There were three of them. The first was for toboggans made out of corrugated iron. The second was for light-weight armour-plating for warships which consisted of hollow triangular steel plates which would be filled with a mixture of cork dust and water through which carbonic acid gas had been forced on the same principle involved in the manufacture of aerated bread. The third patent involved a lightweight version of this armour for the use of infantry soldiers.

On 6 February Mr Chalk addressed a letter of protest to Dr Hyslop, the senior assistant medical officer, in which he denounced his detention as illegal, and threatened court action. On 17 February the notes record that he has been objecting to the night watch and that he had set his water can inside the door of his room so that the attendants carrying out the night watch would stumble over it.

On 7 March he had an idea 'that he, and only he, can reform the Lunacy Act' and told the doctor that he was going to stand for Parliament as a Conservative candidate against Mr Herbert Gladstone at Leeds. He didn't feel that being an undischarged bankrupt would matter as he had several influential friends who would pay off his debts for him. Later in the month, he wrote to the Lunacy Commissioners complaining that he had been assaulted by attendant Steer after playing a game of tennis in the airing court, and that the toilets on his ward were in an unhygenic state. On 13 March he refused to go to bed at night unless Dr Smith was sent for and then threatened one of the attendants with a billiard cue. He was transferred to MIB ward because of this, and because of persistently playing tricks on other patients and putting brooms and other objects out of the windows. His behaviour did not improve. On 15 April he knocked his door with his bed and cracked the attachment of the doorpost to the wall. He was then made to sleep in a strong room with his mattress on the floor. Despite these precautions, on the night of 16 April he refused to go to bed and barricaded himself in the reading room. He reportedly told one of the attendants that he would think nothing of killing Dr Smith. The next day he was discovered to be in possession of a large brass plug from a sink which he had fastened to the end of a belt. On that day he wrote a letter saying that he would not have hesitated to use it as a weapon if necessary to defend himself or while trying to escape, stating that 'I should be within my rights at common law as a freeborn Englishman'. On 20 April he told the staff that he was in possession of half a brick which he would not give up unless allowed to return to Gallery III and to have use of compasses and other mathematical instruments. On 22 April he wrote a letter about his incarceration intended for publication in *The Times*, but it was intercepted by the Hospital. In a subsequent letter to Dr Smith, Chalk made no attempt to mask his contempt for the Physician Superintendent's professional judgement: 'I cannot help expressing my utter astonishment at your idea of preventing me from succeeding in getting my letter of Friday last into *The Times* (though it certainly tends to the future safety and benefit – and I fearlessly await the public verdict upon my suggestions) – in order to prevent my 'succeeding', and thus being elated by success and so remaining what you presume to be 'ill' – in your poor distorted judgement, formed by an experience of lunatics and others – in a narrow professional groove, out of which you seem unable to discern anything among those around you. To attempt to cut down all those within your clutches to the dead level you deem "healthy" is the most diabolical conceit I ever heard of...'

On 28 April he was discovered to have wrenched off two iron window fastenings from which he had made screwdrivers.

This seems to have marked the end of Mr Chalk's attempts to fight his way out of Bethlem. In June, he tried again to send letters to the newspapers stating his case, this time via a fellow patient, John Bishop-Culpepper, who had been granted leave from the Hospital, but these were discovered on Bishop-Culpepper before he left. Mr Chalk also asked Bishop-Culpepper to go to the Mansion House in order to take out a summons against himself, so that Chalk would have to appear in a courtroom and could thereby prove his sanity in public. The plot was discovered upon Bishop-Culpepper's early return from leave (see page 54), and nothing more came of it.

By 4 July things seem to have improved to the point where he was being allowed out of the Hospital with attendants and then on his own so long as he gave his word he would return and would not attempt to engage in any business. These periods of leave were very successful and he was discharged well on 3 August.

A note, added on 18 June 1895, indicates that he came back up to the Hospital wanting to see the original certificate upon which he had been admitted and protesting that he should never have been in the Hospital. He was referred to the Lunacy Commissioners. A final sentence, added by Dr Smith, suggests that Mr Chalk may have become ill again: 'Says he could make a permanent ice-rink here by the use of windmills'.

# 'He recognised that the behaviour of some of the Hospital's patients was peculiar'

**William Cole, a 15-year old boy from Hackney, was admitted on 12 February 1892.**

*Talks in a rambling way, does not realise that an attack he made on a gentleman was wrong. Cannot tell me the day of the month. Talks nonsense about what he has done. His mother, Elizabeth Cole, tells me that he made a violent attack on a gentleman because he looked at him.*

Dr John Langdon Haydon Down, 81 Harley Street, London

*Incessantly talking the greatest nonsense, rambles off one subject to another without any definite reason. His mother, Mrs Cole, states that he strikes matches about the house alight and imagines they are fireworks, pulls the garden up then replaces the earth again, repeatedly doing this.*

Dr Thomas Taylor, 131a Mile End Road, London

Taken on 17 February 1892.

William was said to have always been a very happy child but he had not got on very well at school. Some fifteen months prior to admission he had been concussed after striking his head against an iron bar and had 'never been quite right' since this injury. He had become prone to headaches and feelings of nausea and had begun to do things that were described as silly by his mother. For example, he had brought a quantity of rotten vegetables from Covent Garden to make into pickles, had lit bonfires in the garden and had thrown tiles at his mother when she had tried to extinguish these.

The examining doctor found that he talked fairly intelligently, said that he had come to Bethlem because he was 'bad in the head' and he recognised that the behaviour of some of the Hospital's patients was peculiar. He didn't consider that his behaviour had been unusual and asserted that the man he had struck had struck him first. He denied having thrown tiles at his mother or striking matches around the house but did say that he had been making squibs out of gunpowder. While he answered questions well, he would often laugh in a silly way first but there was no evidence of delusions or hallucinations. The Hospital's governing committee refused to approve his admission, and he left on 19 February.

## 'Yours much damaged'

Taken on 31 March 1893.

**Lynch Maydon, a 55-year old farmer from Mursley in Buckinghamshire, was admitted on 30 April 1892. He had previously been an inpatient at the Hospital from 4 October 1890 to 12 March 1891.**

*Peculiar manner. Lack of concentration. Gait. Tremulous tongue when protruded. Magnificent ideas, money being no object. General appearance and bearing of patient fidgety and restless. Manner excitability and irritability. Unwillingness to go to bed. Desire for alcohol, he usually being very abstemious. Mrs Conway Maydon tells me that he has lost flesh for the past two or three weeks. Has been very irritable and easily raised to anger. Very impatient. Has during past week bought and ordered many expensive things e.g. an American organ and two music stools, two large grain elevators (price £60 each). Instructed contractor to build a Vestry Hall. Has appeared downstairs naked and lain before fire in that state.*

Dr Balfour Neill, Windsor, Buckinghamshire

*Is very restless in manner and seems unable to keep still. Talks indistinctly, his voice is 'thick' and he clips his words. Is unable to carry on a connected conversation. Has had temporary loss of power over certain muscles e.g. of left arm. Is able to 'write all day and work all day' or 'ride all day'. Has extravagant ideas about money matters. By Elizabeth Conway Maydon, that he has lately been running about the fields, walked out into the yard yesterday without his shoes, has lately ordered an organ for his sitting-room and yesterday he ordered (and these articles are not required) 2 elevators, 12 dozen hurdles and a set of harness. Has promised his wife that she may have anything she likes to order and lately ordered a quantity of sacred music of the 'newest' kind.*

Dr George Hanby De'ath, West Street, Buckingham.

His earlier admission had been for an attack of melancholia from which he was considered to have made a good recovery. For three months prior to the current admission he had been abnormally excitable and had become unreliable in his work and with the management of the farm's finances. His diagnosis on admission was of general paralysis and his prognosis given as bad.

Over the following days he remained elated and expansive. He told the doctors that he felt wonderfully happy, quite young again and couldn't remember when he had felt so well. He believed that he had made a lot of money from his farm, particularly from breeding horses and was rich enough to buy anything he wanted. He was very keen to go out of the Hospital and catch a train back to his home and would be very abusive to the attendants if they would not fetch his hat and coat so that he could leave.

On 29 May he was reported to be looking unwell and attributed this to worry at being kept in the Hospital while his business was going to 'rack and ruin' at home. His physical condition and mental state deteriorated so that by August he was noted to have a more shuffling gait and to be weaker in his intellect. On 7 September he wrote a letter protesting his continued detention at Bethlem: 'This is the last appeal I shall make to be set at liberty. I will proceed at once to put the law in motion. You know as well as I do that you have not the smallest right to lock me up here. There has never been a little the matter with me, as you know, and I want to know by what reason or authority you keep me shut up here, away from my home and business.

I shall sue you for very heavy damages as soon as I get out, and I shall at once apply to Mr Lewis to come and liberate me and commence the action against you and Dr Smith. We will ruin your institution and have it shut up which we are quite sure we can do.'

He signed off, 'I remain, yours much damaged, L.C. Maydon'.

On 2 December he had a seizure which left him with paralysis of his left arm. In February 1893 he had a short period of aphasia but recovered from this and was elated again in mood now saying that he would 'stand the whole village a dinner'. Sadly he then began to deteriorate with prolonged fits affecting the left side of his body. By 12 May he was described as becoming very weak with difficulty in swallowing. He gradually became exhausted and died on 17 May.

## 'I am as well now as the day I came into this blessed establishment'

Taken on 27 March 1893.

**Ralph Rolls, a 69-year old retired railway inspector from Clapham, was admitted on 4 May 1892.**

*In conversation he told me he had caught his wife in the very act of being unfaithful to him, but had done nothing to stop it. He also said he had felt children in her stomach, kicking about. They were not his and she had got rid of them by some means. Complained of his food being tampered with by his wife. Rosa Rolls, the wife, tells me that he is very abusive to her, and finds fault with everything she does in consequence of his believing that she is unfaithful to him with any man that comes into the house. Had tried to drown himself.*

Dr Arthur Frederick Loch Dorin, 344 Clapham Road, Clapham

*He is emotional and lacking in self-control. He burst out weeping copiously at the beginning of my interview, but soon changed to laughter. He is deluded and says he is certain that his wife has recently been unfaithful to him and that he detected her 'in flagrante delicto'. He says she became pregnant by a stranger and got rid of the child by stealth. He says his wife drugs his food and on that account he refuses supper. He has signs of organic brain disease; his speech is impaired and his gait feeble.*

Dr John Warnock, Medical Superintendent, Peckham House, Peckham

The first signs of illness had been in July 1891, when his family had noticed that he had become forgetful and was dragging his left foot when he walked. He had seen and heard hallucinations of strange men walking about his house at night and had complained that food prepared for him by his wife had a strange taste. Immediately prior to admission he had threatened to drown himself and had filled a bath and got into it fully clothed to that end. His diagnosis on admission was senile melancholia and his prognosis was described as bad. His physical condition was weak, it being reported that he could not walk more than a few yards without assistance.

By 13 May he was reported to have improved in that he was now eating and sleeping well and had admitted that he must have been mistaken in his ideas about his wife. This improvement was maintained so that on 7 June he was sent to Witley to convalesce. On

5 July he wrote a letter to his 'dear wife' from Witley: 'Read yours of 3rd last. As you say the weather is hot. Sorry to hear you had a bad headache. I sincerely hope it is better. I am sorry I did not ask you how you were but I am afraid I am forgetful and negligent for which I pray your forgiveness. Don't talk to me about my illness being a trial. Bosh, I have not had any illness. I am as well now as the day I came into this blessed establishment. Perhaps I had not better say any more, it might be detrimental to me, don't talk any more about my illness. It is a mystery to me how you got my money. I never authorized anyone to get it. I don't owe any doctor's bill. Give my love to the children and accept the same yourself. How are you this morning?' He dedicated his letter, 'Yours till death, Ralph' and added, 'P.S. Have been blood spitting all night'.

Sadly, he suffered a relapse and was returned to Bethlem on 6 August, by which time his ideas about his wife's infidelity had returned and could not be shifted. In January 1893 there is a report that he will not write to his wife, is hostile to her when she visits and at times will not speak to her. Little else is recorded in his notes until September when he is described as quiet and weak minded with a worsening memory. By then he was doing very little to occupy himself and no longer worried about going home. On 9 October he was transferred to Bethlem's incurable ward. Here he developed chronic kidney disease, and was bed-ridden by February 1895. He was nursed in a water bed to prevent the development of pressure sores, and his friends were informed of his failing health. He finally died on 15 June 1897.

# 'Her friends had been told about the graveness of her condition'

Probably taken in September or October 1892.

**Alice Campion, a 30-year old widow, was admitted on 25 June 1892, having just arrived by ship from Australia.**

*She has loss of memory and cannot remember where she has been since leaving England five years ago. States that she has never seen her nurse before, though she attended her during her voyage from Australia. Cannot remember her own or her sister's name. Annie Cobden of Grays, Essex, stewardess of SS Ophir, states that the patient was constantly pacing the deck for hours together and while doing so would attempt to undress herself or defecate or urinate in public and became extremely violent when prevented.*

Dr Thomas Wholey, 296 Winchester House, Old Broad Street, London

*There was an inability to fix attention, loss of memory and absence of reasoning power. In fact she was unable to give a rational answer to any question I put to her. Communicated to me by Annie Cobden who tells me that the patient is very noisy at times. Refused to remain in bed at night and is continually divesting herself of her clothes and walks her room in a state of nudity.*

Dr Arthur Cæser, 457 Bow Road, London

When she was brought to the Hospital she had been crying out so loudly that this had frightened the horse of the carriage in which she had travelled. Her mental state fluctuated. Some days she would not answer any questions and would pace restlessly about apparently disregarding those around her. On other days she would answer questions and laugh but her answers seemed to be quite random. When questioned she didn't know the day of the week or the year, couldn't recall her own name and thought the Hospital was her home. At times she was highly grandiose and told the doctor that she was 'Princess Nuttall' and had given thousands of pounds to the Hospital and had seen her sister exercising in the airing court. Her speech was noted to be very strange. She would only use one or two words at a time and is described as being like Dingle in *Pickwick Papers*. For example, she would point to her mouth and say 'teeth – beautiful'. By August she was settled in the Hospital and spending her time collecting fallen leaves which she described as 'gardening – pretty'. On 15 November she was described as gradually becoming weaker and more demented though more placid in her manner. On 30 March 1894 she was so weak that she was unable to walk and was crawling about the Hospital. This physical decline continued so that on 15 August she was described as 'very weak physically, dirty and demented'. On 20 November she was reported to be very noisy, shouting out almost continually on alternate days. By 21 February 1895 she was being nursed on a water bed to prevent the development of pressure sores and was incontinent in bed. She was getting very thin but was still eating well. On 7 March the notes record that she was 'slowly dying' and was now unable to take food. Her friends had been told about the graveness of her condition and were visiting her regularly. By 11 March she was unconscious, but still taking milk and brandy, and on 13 March she died.

# 'She made grimaces at me and said that I had been 'Kodaked' by her'

Probably taken in July 1893.

**Georgina Hewett, a 26-year old single woman from St Leonards-on-Sea, Sussex, was admitted on 3 November 1892.**

*She cannot converse in a rational manner. She will not answer questions. She chatters continuously in an incoherent rambling and garrulous way. Spoke of her mother as a devil. She seems quite unable to take care of herself. Her mother, Mrs Jane Hewett (widow), informs me that yesterday the patient exposed herself at the window in a state of nudity and that she has been for some time unable to manage herself and her affairs.*

Dr Francis John Roberts Russell, Tramore, London Road, St Leonards-on-Sea, Sussex

*Her manner is excited, she keeps talking nonsense. She made grimaces at me and said that I had been 'Kodaked' by her. She also said that she had been starved. Alice Hewett, sister, says that she dresses up in fantastic dresses, that she exposes herself at the window in scanty dress, that she uses bad language.*

Dr Edward Rosser Mansell, 44 Wellington Square, Hastings, Sussex

She had apparently been very ill with influenza some 18 months previously and was not felt by her family to have ever been fully well since. A few weeks before the admission a woman had come to stay at the house who bore some resemblance to a male family friend and she had caused some embarrassment by continually asking whether she was him dressed up. She had threatened to kill herself by holding her breath.

When she first arrived at the Hospital she refused food and had to be forcibly fed. On 6 November she struggled so much when the staff were trying to feed her that she had to be fixed into the chair to facilitate this. She would hold her breath until she became cyanosed during this procedure. On 12 November she was 'still very noisy and having to be fed with the tube', but on 14, 17 and 22 November it was noted that she was feeding herself. By 25 November she was having continuous baths for an hour a day but this did not seem to improve her symptoms. Through the winter and spring she continued to be described as getting better physically with marked gains in weight but without any change in her mental state or behaviour. She was discharged uncured on 25 October 1893 and admitted to Redlands, a lunatic house in Tonbridge, Kent.

# 'The family and myself are desirous of having him home'

**George Hake, a 46-year old publican from Upton Park, was admitted on 16 November 1892.**

*His changed conduct and indifference to ordinary surroundings. Dwells only on his own sinful life, believes himself to be persecuted by the devil and never to be forgiven of God. Sees tokens of all kinds in the house of death and the devil – Lucifer matches, ribbons, etc. Picked up a small image and said it was the devil who is in the house and all over the place. Says his wife and family are ruined and will be killed. Talked of taking out the heart of his wife and youngest child who were going above. Was restless, constantly on the move and picking at imaginary things.*

Dr Francis Mead Corner, Manor House, East India Road, Poplar

Probably taken in March or April 1893.

*He said that he had been a great sinner all his life and that there was no hope for him in the next world. Asked his reason for this, he told me that he had received a message from above from his wife whom he declared to have died in the night. The message proved to be his name printed on the corner of his handkerchief.*

Dr Horace George Turney, St Thomas' Hospital, Albert Embankment, London

His illness had begun in May 1891, when he had become quieter than usual and been observed to brood much to himself. He had then sold his business without any apparent reason and in June 1892 had bought a new business in Hastings. This had failed and had to be sold in August with a consequent loss of £2000. He had then become more withdrawn and had started to express ideas that he had ruined his family and that they would be better off dead. He had experienced visual hallucinations and saw the devil's tail coming out of his daughter's pocket and also auditory hallucinations: hearing the sound of horses' hooves and the devil's voice saying 'Got you'. He could feel snakes moving inside himself and had felt the devil take hold of his arm.

Through December 1892 and January 1893 he remained very depressed and deluded, but on 2 February 1893 Dr Maurice Craig, one of the Hospital's clinical assistants, recorded that Hake was improving and now reading. According to Dr Craig, Hake remembered his visions of the devil but was beginning to see that it might have been a delusion. On 21 March, his wife wrote to Dr Smith.

'Sir, Having thought seriously over my husband's condition and finding him so much more rational, the family and myself are desirous of having him home. I will watch over and take every care of him. Therefore I should like to remove him.'

On 12 April, he is described as anxious to go home and although he still says that he believes he is wicked and can remember seeing meaning in everything, he now believes that these were misinterpretations. He was discharged relieved on 17 April.

# 'You are ruining my prospects in the future and blasting my life'

Taken on 22 March 1893.

**Thomas Hayman, a 23-year old clerk to a colonial merchant, from Lee, Kent, was admitted on 11 February 1893.**

*Naturally quiet, sedate and amiable, a few months ago he was the subject of an acute melancholia. Now he has become irritable, excited, exuberant in his actions in singing and talking, extravagant with his money, that he borrows recklessly and that he proposes to repay by eccentric procedures. Quarrelsome with those most dear to him. Remaining out at night running recklessly about on foolish errands. His mother, Charlotte Hayman of 13 Southbrook Road, Lee, Kent, tells me that his treatment of her is most extraordinary and that he is quarrelsome with her although he likes her. He is contemplating marriage with five or six girls, all of whom he knows nothing of and whom he has picked up casually. His brother-in-law, Richard Langford of 6a Old Kent Road states that he orders unnecessary clothing and sends his bills into him, and that he practises masturbation considerably.*

Dr John Sutton Sams, Eltham Road, Lee, Kent

*Patient is very talkative. When asked a question will ramble on to any amount from one thing to another (this is so unlike him as he was always very quiet and reserved in his manner). He will answer any private matter with perfect indifference. He has several ladies he corresponds with, with views to matrimony. He says that he has been spending his money so freely of late because it accumulated when he was sent away to live with a doctor in Eastbourne. By Florence Lilian Hayman, his sister, patient is very untruthful and excited whereas he hardly used to speak. Thinks he has plenty of money and spends a tremendous lot. He says he has five or six girls he is going to marry. He used to be so particular about his dress and now does not care at all.*

Dr Leopold Burroughs, 116 Lee Road, Blackheath

His admission diagnosis was acute mania and his prognosis was given as good. When he entered the Hospital he was in high spirits and was overheard singing 'Mary Jane was a farmer's daughter' in the hall, and was dancing and singing in the Gallery. He signed a request to see a magistrate and then told the doctor that he was going to see a 'beak' the next day, and hoped that the hearing would be in private as he did not want it to be reported in the newspapers. On 28 February it was reported that he was inclined to annoy other patients by calling them names and coughing as he passed them, and on 15 March he is reported to be still excited at times but no longer singing. In that month, he was refused permission to attend the patients' ball by Dr Smith, the Hospital's Physician Superintendent, a course of action which Hayman considered to be 'very mean and ungentlemanly'. On 17

March he wrote a letter to Dr Smith that alternated in tone between angry and pleading: 'I herewith beg to complain of your treatment to me which I consider unkind, unjust and unmanly. In the first place, I am told that it is found impossible to satisfy an outsider that I am insane and yet I'm kept here ... Secondly, by detaining me here you are ruining my prospects in the future and blasting my life, for what firm would employ a young fellow who had been imprisoned in a lunatic asylum? What girl of any spirit or social status would yoke herself for life to a man who had spent some months of his life among idiots?

I ask you the plain and straightforward question "When am I likely to go to Witley and leave this 'abomination of desolation'?" and I must beg of you to give me a correspondingly straightforward answer. There appears to me to be no just cause or impediment to my going to Witley on Tuesday next. If that opportunity is not taken, another fortnight has to be got through. My uncle, who has come up from Cornwall for a week, came to see me last night, and has been staying with one of the partners in my firm, who assured him they would keep my situation as long as they conveniently could, but after six months' absence in the summer, you can imagine how long that will be? What will be the use of seven years' reference? If they give me the sack, you will have the pleasure of lying down to sleep at night firmly convinced that you have done your best, or worst, to ruin a human creature's life, nay that of a fellow man. May the knowledge add to the peace of your slumbers. Had I the same assurance, sleep would be impossible to me, but no doubt my conscience has not yet been sufficiently dulled to the cry of humanity and justice, or my feelings sufficiently seared so as to enable me to act as though I were guiltless of possessing that undesirable (in this century at any rate) part of anatomy known as the heart.

Trusting you will give this matter your earnest attention. What may seem childish to you, and what may savour strongly of "an idiot's tale, full of sound and fury, signifying nothing", is a matter of life and death, bodily and mentally, to me. I am sane, so help me God, and consider myself a man.'

He had 'scuffles' with the attendants on 6 and 23 April, and on 12 May threatened to take legal action against Dr Smith if he was not released from the Hospital. 'You may be a "little tin God on wheels" in your own estimation, but you are a mere unit in the eyes of the English law', he wrote. On 3 June he was improving although still writing 'foolish letters to his lady friends'. He was transferred to Witley on 11 July. He returned on 5 September and was granted leave from the Hospital for a month. This was extended on 4 October and he was discharged well by certificate on 9 November.

On 7 May 1894, Hayman wrote a letter to Dr Smith which suggested that, though his anger at the Hospital had subsided, a residual body of unusual convictions may have persisted. 'I now write to thank you and all the other doctors for the great kindness and consideration shown to me when a patient at Bethlem Royal Hospital ... Dr Savage told me once when addressing his students, with myself as a specimen of "undue exaltation of spirits", that I should not be well until I felt grateful. If such a statement be correct, I must be quite well now as I feel very grateful ... I presume you saw the account in the newspapers of the trial of Dr Sherrard of Eastbourne, and as there is "no smoke without fire", you will no doubt admit that the contents of that letter which I wrote to a friend in Australia, and which you stopped, you will I repeat no doubt agree with me that my epistle was not "an idiot's tale, full of sound and fury, signifying nothing".'

# 'At times clean, at others filthy, always fanciful and decorative in dress'

Taken in July or August 1893.

**Elsie Schmidt, a 30-year old single music teacher from High Barnet, was admitted on 16 February 1893. She had previously been an inpatient at Bethlem from 12 March 1887 to 7 March 1888.**

*Her manner is quite changed. Her conversation is rambling from one subject to another. She is sleepless and very restless. Has used violence to her nurse. Says she hears voices talking to her (which have no existence). Sometimes is laughing, sometimes is crying. Says her head was actually swelled to an enormous size yesterday which was not the case. Daniel Schmidt, tailor, 93 High Street, Barnet (the father of the patient), states that she has been under restraint on two previous occasions. That she locks herself up in rooms and rummages everything all about. She pockets all she can, odd things, hairpins, matches, ornaments, etc. She tears her clothes. She does not sleep, but sings, screams and shouts for long together. She is destructive and has broken up her watch. Is most violent at times and very cunning.*

Dr Thomas Thyne, Wood Street, Barnet, Hertfordshire

*She talked continuously and somewhat confusedly, telling me in a rambling way her previous history, occasionally mixing up events of some years back with those a few weeks ago. Talked excitedly of a case of illness in the neighbourhood and of her own proceedings in cooking and feeding the nurses. Says she has occasionally been suspicious of attempts to poison her and that ether was lately given her in place of brandy a few days ago at New Barnet in a shop. Annie Bailey (professional nurse) says that during the night she has been shouting and dancing about in a state of nudity, calling her a devil and declaring that there are other girls in the room when no-one else was in fact present.*

Dr Reginald John Ryle, Northland, Hadley, Barnet, Hertfordshire

On admission her answers to questions were rambling and difficult to follow. The admitting doctor recorded verbatim extracts of her speech in the casebook to illustrate this. For example, when asked about the visual hallucinations she was reported to have experienced, she said 'As they involved poisons which were earthy which had fulfilled revelations', and about her auditory hallucinations answered 'Where there was marble and jasper which could be produced to life'. She complained that she had seen two great lights and a number of stars in her room and at one point had seen flames coming under the door. She would collect bits of stick and potato in her pockets and produce these for the staff with 'childish pleasure'. Her lack of sleep caused great concern to the doctors and on 23 February it was noted that despite sleeping draughts she had had 'scarcely any sleep since admission'. On 13 March in conversation with the doctor she asked him how much he had given for his cuff links and watch. When he replied that they were presents, she told him that if she were a man she would be ashamed to be dependent and 'unceremoniously turned on her heel and walked away'. She was treated with hyoscine at night, which helped her to sleep for five to six hours each night. Through the summer she remained unpredictable and in June was described as 'at times clean, at others filthy, always fanciful and decorative in dress'.

By November she had improved and was dressing more carefully and considered less eccentric in her manner and behaviour. She attended a Hospital dance and was reported to have behaved well. On 14 February 1894 she was granted three weeks leave. On 24 March she was still generally improved but was still subject to fits of temper and episodes of uncontrollable behaviour. She would tie her hair up in what were described as 'fanciful forms' and had a 'tendency to decorate herself with odd bits of coloured stuffs'. She was formally discharged uncured on 9 May, but did not in fact leave at that time. On 6 June it was noted that her discharge had been rescinded and her time in the Hospital extended by one month. This appears to have been in response to some further improvement in her condition as she was discharged relieved on 4 July.

## 'She called the medical officers by familiar names'

Taken in August or September 1893.

**Serena Grace, a 54-year old housewife from Clapham, was admitted on 6 March 1893.**

*She is very excitable and talks in a rambling manner on religious subjects, states that she has lately been in Heaven for several days and that she is going again in a day or two. She also states that her neighbours and her husband are going to murder her. She also says that during the last week she got several of her neighbours locked in prison to prevent them murdering her. Fanny Scott of 6 Kay Road, Stockwell, no occupation, her sister, informs me that she has the delusion people are coming into her room at night to rob and murder her and that these people can get in through the windows and keyholes.*

Dr William Atkinson, 95 Clapham High Street, Clapham

*She says she is in constant fear of her life owing to certain persons entering her home and using violent threats. Also that the same persons break into her home at night and rob her of money and various articles and that she is obliged to be surrounded by her friends for protection. William John Grace, 17 Abbeville Road, North Clapham, Surrey, says the patient complains that the lodgers on the ground floor are robbing her of her goods and trying to murder her.*

Dr Richard Steven Wallis, 37 High Street, Clapham

She was apparently very violent and excited on admission, but when seen by the doctor the following day was much calmer. She told him that her lodgers, who she believed had stolen from her, had been sentenced to six months on the treadmills and six strokes with the lash by the doctor downstairs, who she believed to be a judge. On 9 March she told the doctor that the man downstairs, who she identified as Mr Pearce, had '100 whores and lots of young girls' and had arranged for her to be brought to Bethlem. She was elated and grandiose, on 20 March declaring that she was 'Lady Grace' and that her husband was Chancellor of the Exchequer. On 6 April she claimed that she was an Empress and daughter of the Queen and that she had given birth to a son that morning. On 9 April she told the doctor that she had given birth to the Lord Jesus Christ the day before yesterday.

She was treated with thyroid gland extract (because her physical appearance had led the doctors to consider myxoedema, an underactive thyroid gland) and with prolonged baths. On 2 June it was noted that she had torn up her clothes while in the bath. On 29 June she said that she was the Princess May and that she was shortly to be married to the

Duke of York – a delusion similar to that later reported by Emma Shearman (see page 95). She was going to the WC with all the other patients, reportedly 'to encourage and aid their efforts', but also harboured darker intentions, such as 'continually wanting to cut someone's head off'.

By 2 October she was described as 'tidier and better' but still alternating between depression and elation. She continued unchanged in this respect. According to a note of 18 January 1894, she called the medical officers by familiar names and was claiming to be the 'direct representative of Christ'. She was discharged uncured on 30 May. There is a final note, dated 25 June, to say that she had become excited again.

# 'Is it all a dream? Am I going to be hurt?'

Taken sometime in 1893 or 1894.

**Kate Trott, a 22-year old single shorthand writer from Westminster, was admitted on 25 March 1893.**

*Loss of memory as to period of time elapsed since recent events. Sayings: 'You have been unkind all you who have mesmerised me', 'You have robbed my grandmother'. She has the delusion that there is danger from police if she goes out of doors. She refers to her mother as 'That woman' and says 'You are not my mother'. The patient's father, Alfred Trott, Draper, 39 York Street, Westminster, says that she has not slept for three nights, but has jumped up constantly in bed wishing to go out to a fire which she sees. She refuses food.*

Dr Albert Ernest Cope, 38 Rochester Row, Westminster

*She is vacant in her manner, tells me that policemen have been waiting outside for her and troubling her for a long time, even when she was at business and that she hears voices of all sorts of people telling her to do wrong. The said patient's father, Alfred Trott, tells me that she refuses food, refuses to go to bed, believes policemen are outside waiting for her and is restless and vacant in her manner.*

Dr William Donald Smallpeice, 42 Queen Anne's Gate, Westminster

Her symptoms had started in December 1892 when she became depressed after not receiving a letter from a gentleman that she had been awaiting. She had gradually lost interest in work and had started getting up later in the mornings. About three weeks prior to admission, she had been playing the piano to accompany three violinists when she had suddenly stopped playing and appeared to fall asleep for half a minute. Her family had sent her on a short holiday, and on her return home she had stayed in bed and would not speak to her family or take food. She had then developed her delusions about the police being after her, and that there were fires in the house. Her diagnosis on admission was resistive melancholia and the prognosis was given as fair.

Following admission she continued to refuse to eat or to dress herself and had to be forcibly fed by nasal tube and dressed by the attendants. When she was questioned by the doctor, she would either repeat his words or ask 'Is it all a dream?' or 'Am I going to be hurt?' She told the doctor that for some weeks prior to admission she had been unable to keep her attention fixed on her shorthand writing and that she had not been able to manage as many words a minute as was usual for her. She complained that she could hear voices and had seen people in her room at night. When asked who she had seen, she indicated some of her fellow patients.

She soon began to eat unaided, but her behaviour remained otherwise unchanged. On 2 April there is a report that she was still very confused and unco-operative, and was tearing and clutching at everything she saw. She had improved sufficiently by the end of the year to be granted leave, and on 20 December leave was granted for one week. However, a note written on 20 January 1894 reveals that further leave was withdrawn because she had told the staff that she would take the first opportunity to do away with herself. She had made sufficient improvement during her admission for the doctor to write that, although her manner remained silent and preoccupied, on the whole she was improved. She was discharged uncured on 20 March.

# 'She wept continuously and refused to speak'

Taken sometime in 1893 or 1894.

**Jane Wheeler, a 24-year old single woman, originally accepted as a voluntary boarder on 15 March 1893, was certified and admitted on 25 March after refusing food for several days.**

*She wept continuously all the time I was with her and refused to speak, except in monosyllables and long intervals. Mary Lulham, attendant at Bethlem Hospital where the patient has been as a voluntary boarder for the past ten days, tells me that she cries frequently, speaks to no-one and for the past two days has utterly refused to take food.*

Dr Horace George Turney, St Thomas' Hospital, Albert Embankment, London

*She sits or stands staring vacantly anywhere. Her countenance is expressive of the greatest misery and helplessness. In conversation she seems unable to give any reason for her condition, absence from friends, etc. Refuses food giving no reason for it. Will stand about in a vacant manner for hours. Communicated by E. Rogers, head attendant, Bethlem Hospital, Female Ward IV.*

Dr Charles Francis Fenton, 31 Linton Road, Barking, Essex

Her earliest symptoms had been observed eighteen months earlier when she had stopped speaking to her mother. It emerged that she had developed a delusion that her mother (who had been widowed six months before) was about to marry again. Three weeks prior to admission she had taken a small bottle of aconite with the intention of poisoning herself. Her diagnosis on admission was chronic melancholia and her prognosis given as bad.

Following admission she had to be tube-fed and there are notes recording this on 26 March and 30 March. By 7 April she was taking food well and not requiring the use of the stomach tube, but she remained depressed and tearful. Through May it was noted that she was working in the gallery and seemed better, but on the morning of 1 June she suddenly became very violent, screaming and kicking at staff, and had to be removed to a padded room. For the rest of her time in the Hospital she alternated between periods of excitement, when she would scream and laugh, and of misery, during which she would remain utterly silent and try to harm herself. For example, on 19 July she tried to choke herself by putting her fingers in her mouth. There are also reports in the notes that she is becoming 'weak minded' and will not do anything for herself. She was discharged uncured on 28 February 1894.

# 'She was becoming tired of waiting for the world to come to an end'

**Annie Cumberbatch, a 30-year old single woman from Brondesbury, was admitted from Bethnal House, a private lunatic house in East London, on 28 March 1893.**

*She stated to me that a month ago she had swallowed a poison, viz. hydrochloric acid, that it had failed to kill her but it had affected all those around her and had rendered the inhabitants of the whole world insane. Walter Henry Southern of 36 Gracechurch Street, EC, solicitor, informs me that she states that all the houses in her neighbourhood are tumbling down and that everyone will be killed.*

James Herron, 73 Southwark Bridge Road, Southwark

*She stated to me that she had taken hydrochloric acid and she had thereby poisoned everyone she had come into contact with. She told me all the houses and all the telegraph wires in London were falling down and that everyone but herself was mad. Walter Henry Southern informs me that she states that people are coming to fetch her and take her away to punish her for having poisoned all the people in the world.*

Dr Charles Cochrane Dickson, Bownant House, Willesden Lane, London

Taken in the Hospital's airing court sometime in 1893.

Her diagnosis on admission was melancholia and her prognosis given as fair. In her previous history she was reported to have always been of 'weak intellect' and to have been seduced by a 'man of position' while she had been in Germany. She had an illegitimate child living, but there is no reference anywhere in the casebook as to whether she had kept this child. Following admission she continued to express her fears that the world was about to come to an end and that she had poisoned people around her. Despite these delusions, she appeared to be more cheerful and on 4 May was reported to be playing tennis and to seem improved. Her fears of being taken away for punishment appear to have persisted. She gave Hospital staff a list of four or so trusted people who might be allowed to visit her, and instructed them not to permit any other visitor to see her. Blanche Cumberbatch, the patient's sister, was not on this list, and was initially refused permission to visit. However, the Lunacy Commissioners took up her case, and in June instructed the Hospital to allow her to visit.

By 16 June, Annie Cumberbatch was well enough to play a piano duet with Dr Smith as part of a Hospital concert programme. On 1 October she told the doctor that she was becoming tired of waiting for the world to come to an end, and by 13 November was reported to have lost all her delusions. She told the staff that she did not believe that the world was actually coming to an end at the present time, although she still entertained the possibility that 'it may do so'. On 15 November she was granted a month's leave and was discharged well on 13 December 1893.

# 'She had a divine mission to crush socialism'

Taken sometime in 1893.

**Julia Scott, a 29-year old mother's help from Regent's Square, was admitted on 28 March 1893.**

*Strangeness of manner. Intense excitement. Tells me she had a divine mission to crush socialism. Says that she is dying and orders me out of the room so that she may die in peace. The father, Herbert William Scott, tells me she insists for the Saviour to be sent for as she has recently seen him. She walks about the house in her nightdress and is perfectly unmanageable.*

Dr Richard Paramore, 2 Gordon Square, London

*The patient refuses to answer any questions whatever. She casts her eyes up and throws herself into unmeaning attitudes. Her father, Herbert William Scott of 4 Regent Square, insurance agent, tells me that the patient states that she has a divine mission from Christ himself whom she is in* communication with. She attempted to throw herself out of the window under the impression that Christ would come for her. She raves incoherently.

Dr William Sinclair Cameron, 201 Grays Inn Road, London

She had first become unwell about two months earlier when she had started alternately laughing and crying in a state of excitement. She had made a very serious attempt to jump out of a seventh floor window on 27 March and had told her family that she wanted people to see her die so that they might know how to die properly themselves. Her diagnosis at admission was given as acute mania and her prognosis as fair.

On 22 April, Charles Mercur, a doctor by profession, wrote to the Hospital passing on the following details: 'Julia Scott was housemaid to my mother who asked me to see her, the direct result of my visit being her transference to Bethlem. From communications made by my mother to my wife, I should fancy that there is strong reason to suspect the existence of pregnancy. Further than this I have no detailed knowledge of the case.'

Following admission she was described as 'dramatic' in her manner and would throw herself about the ward or stand in an attitude of prayer for extended periods. She refused food, but could be fed with a spoon by staff. By 27 April, she had been moved to FIA ward, and was described as being very dirty in her habits and not speaking or opening her eyes. By 3 June she was being fed by tube, but on 27 June it was noted that she had been taking food for three days and was now much better. She was keeping her eyes open more but remained dirty in her habits.

On 11 August she had her first menstrual period since her illness had begun, and the idea that she might have been pregnant was abandoned. She was still doing strange things such as taking bits to eat out of the ashtray. On 25 August she was described as much improved, and was transferred to Witley the following week. She returned on 26 September and was discharged well.

# 'A terrible awful doom in front of her'

**Ella Badger, a 20-year old single woman from Hillsborough in Sheffield, was admitted on 15 April 1893.**

*She is restless, walking about her room, talking at times incoherently. She is under the impression that she should not eat. During the time I made my examination, she was walking around her room, quietly but aimlessly. She is suffering from melancholia. Letitia Badger, her mother, says that she has threatened suicide. They have difficulty getting her to walk in the garden and as great a difficulty in getting her into the house again.*

Dr James Holmes, 55 Harcourt Road, Sheffield, Yorkshire

*Said 'I will do it'. Refuses food. Refuses to talk or answer when spoken to by me. She volunteers that she is dreadfully wicked and ought to die. 'Can't do anything to get a living and is no use in the world'. By Mr Andrew Badger and Mrs Letitia Badger, 'At first my daughter was saying continually that she was going to die and now she says that there is nothing but a terrible awful doom in front of her'.*

Dr Edwin Whitfield Dawson Kite, Hillsborough, Sheffield, Yorkshire

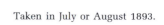

Taken in July or August 1893.

On 2 January a board had fallen six or seven feet onto her head resulting in her being concussed for some little time. After a couple of days she appeared to have made a full recovery, but in February had become restless and 'strange' and had needed to be restrained. When her doctor had been called he had diagnosed 'brain fever' and had confined her to bed. This had seemed to pass off although she had remained incoherent in her speech, intermittently excited and was refusing food. She had spoken to her family about throwing herself out of a window and on one occasion had run up the stairs as if she was going to do this.

Following admission she remained agitated and difficult to communicate with. On 20 April she was reported to be tearful and very unhappy, at times appearing confused so that she had to be assisted with washing and dressing. Her sleeplessness was repeatedly mentioned in the notes until the end of June when she was reported to be sleeping better. On 5 August she was thought to have gradually improved to the point where she had begun to take an interest in her surroundings. On 18 October she was granted one month's leave and was discharged well by certificate on 15 November.

## 'There was a great deal of screaming'

Taken in Hospital's airing court, probably in August or September 1893.

**Alice Meek, a 20-year old unmarried cashier, was admitted from Springfield Hospital in Tooting (which had been Middlesex County Lunatic Asylum since 1889, and was previously Surrey Asylum) on 15 April 1893.**

*She sits with her head down and looks very depressed and miserable, will not answer any questions or replies only in monosyllables and in a very low tone and cries. When I ask her if she is afraid, she says 'Yes', but I cannot get her to state what she is afraid of. Augusta Harries, attendant, Middlesex County Asylum, states that Alice G. Meek rarely says anything, will sit in the same place till moved and when in the airing court stands by herself taking no notice of anything and at times has to be washed.*

Dr Frederick Henry Ward, Senior Assistant Medical Officer, Middlesex County Asylum, Tooting

*She was depressed and dull. Would not speak, only nodded her head when spoken to. She sat staring at the ground and took no interest in anything.*

Dr Hugh Gardiner Hill, Medical Superintendent, Middlesex County Asylum, Tooting

From April to July 1892 she had been working very long hours in a restaurant, reportedly from 8 a.m. to 11 p.m., without opportunity to take breaks for meals. Her father had taken her away from this situation, but it was thought that she had become depressed soon after. By Christmas 1892 she was sleepless and would spend her nights crying, insisting that she had been wicked. She was admitted to Springfield Hospital, Tooting, in February 1893, where she had to be forcibly fed and had not improved.

On admission to Bethlem, she would only answer questions in a monosyllabic whisper, but managed to tell the admitting doctor that she was frightened that something bad was going to happen to her as punishment for her sins. She believed that the staff could read her thoughts and knew about her preoccupations and explained that she therefore didn't believe there was any point in talking to them. She told the admitting doctor that the staff had been very cruel at Tooting, but when asked to elaborate on this would only say 'that there was a great deal of screaming'.

Through April and May she remained very depressed and would not talk to staff, but her mood lifted considerably in the summer. On 27 July it was noted that she was now inclined to be excited, making 'gushing remarks', and was now quite happy. On 9 August she was writing letters with a view to carrying on flirtations with old lovers, and was rushing around the ward in a restless way. On 1 November there is a note that she 'writes poetry and makes sketches (both badly)'. Sadly, none of this work was preserved by the Hospital. Her mood returned more closely to normal in January 1894. On 26 January there is a note to say that over the last few weeks she has slowly improved. She was less noisy but still had an 'excess of spirits' and if crossed, or not allowed her own way, became abusive and lost control. By 20 February she was reported to be much quieter, and she was granted leave for a week on 20 March. She was discharged well on 27 March, but was admitted for a second time on 16 July 1894, and discharged uncured 26 June 1895.

## 'His great trouble is that he ought to have been a musician'

Taken on 1 May 1893.

Alfred Broughton, a 42-year old compositor from
Kennington Park, was admitted on 27 April 1893.

*He told me that last November he had a vision which he attempted to describe. Since then he said that he had lost all interest in or love for life. When he heard people talking he always feared that they were saying something about him. He had recently meditated suicide by means of poison. Mary Ann Broughton, wife of the above, tells me that her husband had an attack of great violence last November and since then has been intensely suspicious of all about him. He has secreted razors presumably with the idea of suicide.*

Dr Horace George Turney, St Thomas' Hospital, Albert Embankment, London

*Says he is anxious to get out of the world but is afraid to take his life. Cannot set his type as he used to do as he mixes up the letters. His great trouble is that he ought to have been a musician.*

Dr Ewen Carthew Stabb, St Thomas' Hospital, Albert Embankment, London

His symptoms were thought to have begun a year before. He had become irritable and worried about trivial business matters. He had been confused and suspicious that his workmates were talking against him. In November he had locked up all the razors in the house because he was afraid he might injure his wife and she had become anxious that he would harm himself. His admission diagnosis was melancholia and his prognosis was given as fair.

Following admission he remained depressed, anxious and restless but was not considered to be suicidal. His condition worsened in the summer and he became deluded, on 8 August telling the doctor that he believed he had no liver, that his bowels had stopped working and that the last time he had been to the lavatory he had passed his own windpipe. On 15 August he told the doctor that he had passed his heart. He remained in this miserable state for several months. On 26 March 1894 he refused food, saying that it would do him no good. When the nasal tube was fetched he then took his food himself. On 25 April he was given a three month extension to his admission but this seems not to have been effective in changing his mental state and he was discharged uncured on 25 July.

# 'She had called on friends and relatives without wearing a bonnet'

Taken sometime in 1893 or 1894.

**Emma Lane, a 42-year old married woman from Tottenham, was admitted on 13 May 1893.**

*She imagines that she is a musician and intends giving entertainments, having at the same time no idea of harmony. She says she is pregnant and will be confined next month. She was on the Cricket Ground and came up to me and conducted herself in a strange manner, digging her elbow into my side and going out to talk to the cricketers while out in the field, giving a general invitation to people to go and have tea with her. Mr J. Blower says she told him she was about to purchase the cricket field and the next field to it to give to the unemployed. Mr Lane, her husband, tells me she goes about purchasing quantities of useless articles.*

Dr Edwin John Sykes, 170 West Green Road, South Tottenham

*Patient tells me she is quite sure she is pregnant and is to be confined in July, although she has no symptoms of such a condition and has been twenty years married without having once been pregnant. She has spoken to the nurse about attending to her. Mrs Anne Lane, mother of the patient's husband, tells me that every night she gets up and cooks food for herself, eats but a little of it and mixes the rest with the food for the family next day. When not cooking she is generally writing love letters.*

Dr Edward Hooper May, High Cross, Tottenham

The admission notes gave further details of her behaviour over the preceding weeks. She had spent all her savings from the previous twenty years, and had bought a shop, together with stock to fill it. She had booked a room in which to give a piano recital and had also corresponded with the Alhambra and Empire Theatres with a view to appearing in them. She had called on friends and relatives without wearing a bonnet, and had been up at night preparing strange meals with cucumbers and sweet cheese. Her delusion that she was pregnant had led her to order all kinds of baby linen articles.

Following admission, she was quiet on the wards, but continued to claim that she was pregnant with twins and could feel them moving within her. On 20 September it was noted that all her delusions had gone and she felt better. Upon this improvement, she was allowed leave from the Hospital to visit her family, first for a day, then for a weekend. After the second visit, her husband, Henry Lane, wrote an account of her behaviour at home to Dr Smith, the Hospital's Physician Superintendent, saying that 'although she has much improved, there is a great deal to be desired'. 'I am anxious to see her resume her old place,' he concluded, 'but fear that she is not yet well enough'. On 5 December she was reported to be somewhat exalted. At a Hospital dance she had been 'gushy and free and easy' and it was decided that she should not be allowed to go to the next one. On 20 December she was given a week's leave of absence to spend Christmas with her husband. This leave did not go smoothly. There were complaints that she had been 'giving trouble'; for her part, she admitted only that she had 'just bought a few things'. She continued to be given periods of leave through February and March 1894. On her return from one of these on 30 March, it was reported that she had all sorts of strange sexual feelings. She was granted further leave on 2 May, but did not improve.

On 19 May, her husband wrote again to Dr Smith: 'After having had my wife at home from the Hospital for a fortnight, I beg to furnish you with the result of my observations upon her state. The apparent delay in sending my report has arisen from the hope that she would improve by a longer stay. In that I have been greatly disappointed, her condition showing no improvement whatever. To my mind, the surroundings here are of a nature to please and comfort, quiet indoors, no noisy neighbours, an unusually large garden for a suburban residence, books and magazines in abundance. Although at one time a great reader and industrious gardener, she now seems indifferent to all around her. Any interest when roused is of short duration. Whilst frequently changing her illusions she falls back upon many of her old ones. Having carefully watched allows me to state that she sits in a depressed state for rather long periods, complains of sleeplessness and pains, difficult to get her to take her meals. When she does break silence it is often to the effect that the spirits told her to do this or that. She has revived the tack about having a child, and from that has arisen a strange change of delusions. She imagines that in putting up a window blind that she has injured herself and child, and that she is not to be disturbed, that she must sit still, and one day stayed in bed, that she is going to have an operation and that a doctor is coming to fetch her. The last idea has been so strong that for four days past she has said little else than the cab was coming at ten or eleven, or shifting the time as the day went on. Although seemingly helpless she has been at times obstinate, and will want to go out, making it difficult to control her. I may add that all she has had to drink, beyond beer at meals, has been a little port wine and that of low strength. I profoundly wish that I had reason to report more favourably of my wife, especially as she had so much improved under your kind supervision. These circumstances compel me to further encroach upon your consideration, at least until you determine what shall be done, and I therefore beg to be allowed to bring her to the Hospital on Monday morning next.'

On 23 May she was discharged uncured, but on 30 May her discharge was rescinded and she was readmitted as a private patient. She was not given further periods of leave during the summer and autumn and she was reported to be restless and talking incessantly. She was granted a week's leave on 19 December again to spend Christmas with her family, but was finally discharged uncured on 30 January 1895.

There is a final note in the casebook dated January 1896 to say that the Hospital had received news that she was by then bed-ridden with paralysis and fits and was apparently suffering general paralysis of the insane.

## 'She threatens and strikes the nurses and declares that she will kill them'

Taken sometime in 1893 or 1894.

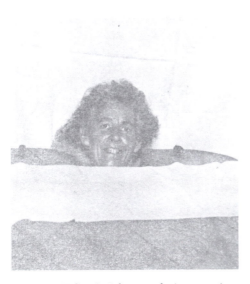

Taken in July 1893 during a session of prolonged bath treatment.

**Emily Crichton, a 37-year old widow from Brighton, was admitted on 19 May 1893.**

*She is incoherent in her conversation and indecent in her remarks. Also regardless of cleanliness and decency in her acts. Violent and threatening to her attendants. Louisa Mohrmann informs me that Mrs Crichton endeavoured to bite her, has been indelicate in her remarks, and acts regardless of decency and cleanliness.*

Dr Patrick Butler, 22 Duke Street, Portland Place, London

*She is suffering from acute mania as indicated by her inability to answer questions rationally, rapid incoherent talking, laughing wildly, without any occasion. I am informed by Miss Annie Johnson that she threatens and strikes the nurses and declares that she will kill them.*

Dr Alfred Lewis Galabin, 49 Wimpole Street, Cavendish Square, London

This was her fourth episode of mental illness. Eight years earlier she had first become ill immediately following the birth of a child. A second 'attack' had followed her husband's death and the third episode had been a year prior to this admission when she had become anxious about her children after they had not returned home at the time she was expecting them. The current episode of illness had begun when she had a miscarriage and related infection. She had become very restless and agitated and had had to be tied down to her bed. On admission she was initially calm but would begin to shout and strike out in an unpredictable manner. She told the admitting doctor to be careful not to tread upon her dead child which was at her side. On 23 May she was reported to still have a raised temperature. She was still very abusive and obscene in her language. On 30 May she had a rigor and her temperature was 102.7 degrees Fahrenheit. Her diet was recorded as: Breakfast, eggs and milk; Lunch, beef tea and eggs; Dinner, fish, custard pudding and milk; during afternoon, milk; Tea, egg and milk; Supper, arrowroot or egg and milk; during the night, milk or cream.

By 18 June she was going out into the Hospital's female airing court, where apparently she would push the other patients about, and was still very excited. On 4 July she was described as better, and was receiving prolonged baths. The baths were stopped on 19 July and she was considered to be much better, although still restless and uncertain in herself. On 30 January 1894 she was transferred to Witley and returned on 27 March. She was discharged well on 28 March.

## 'Approached one of the clinical assistants to ask if he was going to cut off her head'

Taken in the Hospital's airing court sometime in 1893 or 1894.

**Emma Shearman, a 22-year old nurse from Poplar, was admitted on 31 July 1893.**

*She wanted to know 'why she couldn't get rid of the people?' Swaying to and fro and asking 'what had she done?' Wild staring vacant look, then prolonged silence with a repetition of the former phrases and calling for her mother. On 25 July I heard her say often 'that it was all her own wickedness'. Woodley Shearman (mother of the above) says 'wild look, shrieking at night, attempting to throw herself over the stairs'.*

Dr Thomas Power, Arundel House, 156 East India Road, Poplar

*Inactive and silent. Fancies that she is considered very wicked and that she is suspected of having committed some great evil for which she cannot be forgiven. Information given by mother of patient is that she is inactive and silent contrary to her nature. Fancies she is suspected of wickedness by others. Did not want to go to bed last night and wants to be left alone in a room and wants to get possession of a rope, probably for suicidal purposes. Tried to throw herself downstairs.*

Dr Albert Corner, Manor House, 152 East India Road, Poplar

Her admission diagnosis was melancholia and her prognosis described as good. On admission she told the doctor that when she had returned from a short holiday in Yarmouth, people had told her that she was Princess May and that there had been no Royal Wedding because she had been away from London. (On 6 July 1893, Princess May, or Mary of Teck, had married George, the Duke of York, who reigned as George V from 1910 to 1936.) Shearman believed that she had been mesmerised, and that the strange things she had believed or acted upon had been the result of influence over her. Prior to admission she had had a headache, but this was now improved and she attributed this to the beneficial effect of some batteries that were in the Hospital. She continued to be deluded over the following weeks. On 25 August she was reported to have approached Dr Craig, one of the Hospital's clinical assistants, to ask if he was going to cut off her head, and on 1 September she mistook Dr W.H.R. Rivers, a former clinical assistant visiting the Hospital, for her father.

On 27 January 1894 there is a note that she is 'now quite bright and cheerful' and has lost her delusional ideas and suicidal impulses. She was transferred to Witley on 30 January and returned to Bethlem on 27 March to be granted a month's leave. This appears to have been successful and she was discharged well on 25 April.

## 'Appears to know what is going on'

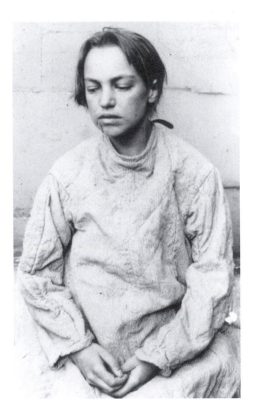

Taken on 30 August 1895.

**Theodora Weston, a 23-year old single woman from Euston Square, was admitted on 28 July 1894.**

*She is in a state of dementia and will scarcely reply to my questions. She says however that she asked if her food at dinner today was poisoned. The aspect yesterday when I saw her was one of suspicion and her manner very reticent. I consider her dangerous to herself. She is restless and wanders about. I am informed by her sister, Miss Ruth Weston, that she has hallucinations, fancying that people are outside to whom she makes signals and with whom she converses. That she required the windows to be closed to prevent people coming in to seduce her. Also that she has tried to leave the house early to go and meet people that she could hear whistling to her. That she refuses food under the idea that it is poisoned.*

Dr Thomas Claye Shaw, Medical Superintendent, London County Council Asylum, Banstead, Surrey

*Patient told me that she would not take her dinner today as she believed it was poisoned and that last night she is sure a man entered her bedroom. She is very suspicious and depressed and said 'Sin is horrible'. Her sister informs me that lately the patient has often refused food and has suspected her sister of trying to poison her. That she has tried to get out to meet imaginary people and has declared that men have entered her bedroom at night, although her sister has always slept in the room with her and assures her that it is untrue.*

Dr William Francis Umney, 15 Crystal Palace Park Road, Sydenham

Her earliest symptoms had been in April 1894 when she had started to tell her family that she believed her food was being poisoned. A sea voyage had been recommended and this seemed to have driven away these ideas temporarily. She had returned to London on 20 July, but her appetite for food had become poor and then the problems detailed in the medical certificates had begun. Her admission diagnosis was melancholia and her prognosis was given as bad.

On admission she was co-operative and would converse sensibly on most subjects, but if asked about her mental condition would refuse to answer. She would not eat and so was fed by means of a nasal tube. On 20 September she told the staff that she felt well enough to go home, but two minutes later struggled and tried to prevent one of the attendants from entering the dining room with the midday meal. In the autumn she became more withdrawn and her behaviour was increasingly unpredictable. By March 1895 she was reported to be very violent at times and was having to be almost constantly watched by the staff. In May she was described as 'now quite demented', although a note dated 5 June records that she 'appears to know what is going on'. On 29 July she began to be treated with prolonged baths, initially for an hour a day, but increasing by an hour each day, so that by 4 August she was bathing for seven hours daily. The baths were discontinued when it was discovered that she had developed marked abrasions on her back and shoulders by rubbing herself against the bath. She was discharged uncured on 21 August 1895 and transferred to Peckham House, a private lunatic house in South London.

There is a final note, dated 31 August 1895, to say that the scars on her shoulders are now healed, and that some marks on her buttocks and left knee are of long standing.

# 'She cannot do things as she feels all in a muddle'

Taken in late August 1895.

**Mary Stoate, a 22-year old single woman from Portman Square, was admitted on 9 February 1895. She had previously been an inpatient at Bethlem from 28 July 1893 to 20 December 1893.**

*Mental depression, absence of self-control, unreasoning irritability, incorrect statements. Her sister, Mrs Green, 78 East Street, Baker Street, W, informs me that Mary Stoate performs indecent and unseemly acts, is changed in character, is sleepless and absent in manner.*

Dr Montagu Handfield Jones, 35 Cavendish Square, London

*She is frequently sighing and depressed and can give no reason for it. She tells me 'she cannot do things as she feels all in a muddle'. Cannot sleep at night. Her expression is heavy and dull, has but little control over her emotions – while talking to me several times burst out laughing at nothing. Sarah Turner, Bethlem attendant, tells me patient is extremely restless, cannot give her attention to anything, was constantly jumping in and out of bed last night. Has been here before and is quite different in appearance and behaviour from what she is when well.*

Dr William Francis Umney, 15 Crystal Palace Park Road, Sydenham

She had suffered with recurrent depression and mania since the age of fourteen. Initially she had become depressed and unable to do her schoolwork. As she grew older the attacks had become more severe so that she would become very depressed, silent and apparently unable to understand what was going on around her.

Following admission she remained restless and distracted. As the admitting doctor tried to question her she would suddenly get up and go to sit on another chair while laughing to herself. Her condition did not change in the first few weeks, but by 10 June she had been transferred to FIA ward because of her tendency to smash things. On 8 July she was no better and beginning to show signs of dementia. She was observed to stand in a corner of the ward most of the day and to pick at her head and neck. On 5 August it was reported that she has pulled nearly all the hair out of her head. Her hair rubbing and pulling continued. On 27 October the doctor recorded that the loss of hair was now confined to the right side of her head, and that there was a clearly defined margin to the area of hair loss. She made no progress over the following weeks and was discharged uncured on 5 February 1895.

There was a happier final entry made in the casebook. A note dated 16 March 1896 says that Mary Stoate had been up to the Hospital and was now quite well.

# 'Her nights were passed in that sweat of death and agony of body and soul'

**Marie André, a 30-year old married woman, was admitted from Holloway Sanatorium, a private asylum at Virginia Water, Surrey, on 21 March 1895.**

*Acute maniacal excitement, raving conversation, incoherent aspect and general appearance that of a lunatic.*

Dr Lyttleton Stewart Forbes Winslow, 33 Devonshire Street, Portland Place, London

*Her appearance is untidy. There is great mental confusion. She can give no proper account of herself and her memory of the events of the past few days is a blank. She is apparently recovering from a state of acute mania.*

Dr William Wadham Floyer, Egham, Surrey

Taken on 27 September 1895.

Her admission diagnosis was puerperal mania and the prognosis was thought to be poor because her condition had already become chronic. She had given birth to a male child in September 1893 but the baby had only lived for sixteen hours. She was unsure of the cause of death but told the Bethlem doctor that the baby had 'spat blood'. She believed that her baby had been killed by a nurse who had put pins down his throat and attributed her psychiatric problems to the shock and distress caused to her by his loss. She told the doctor that she could not sleep at night in the Hospital because the staff persecuted her with 'vapour baths' so that her nights were passed 'in that sweat of death and agony of body and soul'.

On 27 March 1895 she told the staff that she believed that they were all detectives, that she knew where Jack the Ripper could be found and that she knew the house in which a recent Southwark murder had taken place. She remained in very much the same condition and would strike other patients when she was excited. On 22 April she picked up a piece of glass and drew it across her throat, but apparently without causing herself any serious injury. In June it was noted that she continued to use very bad language and had assaulted nurses and patients. She was discharged uncured on 2 October 1895 and was transferred to Peckham House, a private lunatic house in South London.

# 'Considered sufficiently suicidal to remain on twenty-four hour observation'

Taken in August 1895.

**Ralph Dennis, a 19-year old draper's assistant from Weymouth, was admitted on 4 April 1895.**

*Has all kinds of delusions, believes he had rupture of the stomach and internal haemorrhage some three years ago. Consulted, at his own wish, four different medical men and thinks he is now suffering from their not treating his case rightly. Also that they are in league to deceive him as to his real condition of health. Imagines that his heart does not act and that he has no pulse. Also that he has twitching of the mouth which he says is a sign of his early death. Rambling and incoherent in his talk and says his case is hopeless and that he shall be driven to take his life. Reverend E.C. Bennett, 10 Newberry Terrace, Weymouth, Unitarian Minister, says he is unable to talk without always reverting to the various diseases he has had. Says he is suffering from Bright's disease, diabetes and other complaints. Very morbid in his ideas and says he feels inclined to drown himself. Fearfully depressed as to his future state after his death and says his parents and friends wish him to die.*

Dr Thomas Howard Brocklehurst, Hope Villa, Weymouth, Dorset

*He has an anxious and restless look and watches me furtively. He tells me that his soul is lost and that he will burn in hellfire. That his internal organs are injured by a strain received three years since. That his heart does not beat. That he will die this evening. That he feels he will be obliged to destroy himself. That he has diabetes and consumption and is too weak to stand. That his former doctor knows nothing.*
*He has told me all this since I have seen him last November. He was then and is now in perfect bodily health. Alfred Dennis, his father, of Southcliffe, Wyke, Weymouth, tells me that on 24 March he declared he was dead. That previously he had threatened to kill his mother and destroy himself more than once. That he declares always that he is suffering from diabetes and consumption and that his soul is condemned to perdition and his doctors are trying to kill him.*

Dr Benjamin Browning, 16 Royal Terrace, Weymouth

On the night following his admission he made a great noise and had to be taken to one of the downstairs wards. He said that he had done this because he wanted to see his father and was distressed that his father had left him in the Hospital. He repeated his hypochondriacal concerns to the doctor and told him that he believed he had Bright's disease and consumption because he was passing a greater amount of urine than usual, and that he believed he had diabetes because he had noticed a sediment in his urine. On 20 April he was reported to believe that he had been sent to Bethlem as a punishment for doing something wrong. He was considered sufficiently suicidal to remain on twenty-four hour observation until at least 15 June, though by this time he was thought to be reading more and to be less hypochondriacal. Unfortunately he failed to make any further improvement and was discharged uncured on 10 July and transferred to Dorset County Lunatic Asylum near Dorchester.

## 'His screaming attacks were "a species of prayer"'

Taken in July 1895.

**Walter Houghton, a 33-year old builder from Stroud Green, was admitted on 4 April 1895.**

*That he is suffering from an aggravated form of religious mania. He tells me that he feels his life is in his own hands and that if he could throw it off and go into the spirit world he should be quite saved. He says he has since his married life not acted as a Christian and that he must get away from his wife and live alone and he should be right. He also told me that he broke two pairs of spectacles in pieces because they hindered his salvation. His statements all bear on this religious state and are irrational and I am convinced he has a suicidal tendency under this delusion. I am informed by his brother, Arthur Houghton, that on 10 February last he attempted to drown himself in the Dock Basin and was fished out with a boat hook. He was taken before a magistrate and the friends were then advised to place him under restraint. His wife tells me that for many weeks he has been very sleepless, never getting more than from two to four hours sleep of a night. He then rises and spends hours on his knees moaning and shouting till he becomes quite rigid and forbids her to touch him because it would spoil the effect. She tells me also that he threw away his purse and keys onto some waste railway ground.*

Dr William Dingley, 277 Camden Road, London

*Patient is depressed and began to cry while talking to me. He tells me that he is worried about his inner and deeper feelings and religious affairs. That he hears the voice of God through his conscience and feelings and that he has thought God does not want him to live. William Dimond, Bethlem attendant, tells me the patient has had noisy screaming attacks like hysterical fits lasting some minutes since admission here and holds his head back sometimes until he gets blue in the face from his collar.*

Dr William Francis Umney, 15 Crystal Palace Park Road, Sydenham

Before admission he was reported to have been depressed about business matters since Christmas 1894, but nothing particularly worrying had been noticed by his family until Sunday 10 February 1895. After leaving home in the morning he had written a letter to his wife from Camden Town railway station in which he declared that he couldn't stand his life any more and that he had been wicked. He made a will at the station, which he asked a railway official to witness for him. He took a train to Poplar and wired his wife to tell her he had arrived there. He then jumped into the Thames, but was seen and fished out by a group of dock workers. When he was seen by a magistrate after this incident, he seemed quite well and was taken to see Dr Henry Maudsley, who recommended that he was sent to a convalescent home in Matlock for a week. He then was forced to return to his work because of pressure of business. He remained depressed and agitated, convinced that he was unworthy of his wife, that the devil was following him about and that he would have to give his life away in order to avoid eternal damnation.

His admission diagnosis was melancholia and his prognosis given as good. In the days following admission, his behaviour was difficult to manage. While the doctors were doing their rounds he was observed to lean against a wall and throw his head back, moaning in a louder and louder manner until he was making a noise that was described as 'deafening'. During this outburst he held his arms out in a rigid fashion and arched his back. After a few minutes he became quiet and would stand in an unresponsive state. If the doctors stimulated him in any way (they tried tickling him), he would begin to shout again. In between his 'attacks' he would talk normally and play the piano. A few days after admission he told the doctor that his screaming attacks were 'a species of prayer' and was observed in the throes of one of these attacks in the men's airing court. On 7 April he hurt himself by rushing head-first into a wall. This resulted in a wound on his head, which, while only one and a half inches long, was deep and had gone down to the bone. As soon as this had been sutured and dressed by the doctor he jumped up and attempted to dash his head into the wall again. He was restrained from doing so by two attendants. He was then put into a padded room and strong dress put on him. The following day, as the doctors were again on their rounds on the ward, he dashed against the wall again and was then ordered to have two attendants constantly with him. He slept in side arm dress and had a special attendant with him all night. He told the staff that he couldn't resist his impulses to rush at the walls, but the doctors noted that he only did this at 'such times as the attendants are calculated to be most occupied'.

On 10 May he was described as 'still very impulsive and suicidal'. He required the constant special attention of two attendants night and day and would often strike these attendants. Through May and June he frequently had to be force-fed by tube. On 26 June he was discharged uncured for what the Hospital described as 'special reasons'. However, his discharge was rescinded before it took effect because in the days leading up to his discharge he had begun to show some improvements in his sleep, feeding and suicidal tendencies. On 29 July it was reported that he was continuing to improve and was now enjoying a daily plunge bath. He told the doctors that his refusal of food and desire to do away with himself arose from 'religious principles' and that these delusions had now quite gone. By 12 August he was being allowed to go out with his friends and was transferred to Witley. He returned from Witley on 15 October, having stayed on there for longer than was usual at his own request. He was discharged well on 16 October 1895.

## 'He recognised that his year in the Hospital was nearly up'

Taken in August 1895.

John Harley, a 35-year old chief officer with the P&O
Steam Ship Company, was admitted as a certified patient
on 25 April 1895, having been a voluntary boarder in the
Hospital since 23 November 1894.

*He is in a condition of intense misery and is constantly moaning under the weight of this. So wrapt up is he in his wretchedness that he will not readily answer questions. He thinks however that some terrible evil is impending, the nature of which he cannot define. So overwhelmed is he that he wishes himself out of the world. William Reddaway, Bethlem attendant, states that the patient is depressed and unhappy. Constantly wringing his hands and believing that something terrible is going to happen. He refuses food and wishes himself dead. Does not sleep.*

Dr S.G. Toller, St Thomas' Hospital, Albert Embankment, London

*Suspicious of persons – extreme depression. Thinks that he will die shortly and go to the 'lower regions' as he believes that he has led a very wicked life. Thinks he has some severe disease affecting the abdomen and that food does him no good. Bethlem attendant Hobbs states that he refuses to take food, that he imagines he has some severe disease of the abdomen.*

Dr Edward Arthur Saunders, St Thomas' Hospital, Albert Embankment, London

He had been transferred from voluntary boarder status following his refusal to eat and was fed with a tube following his certification. He told the staff that he could not swallow and would shout and struggle when the staff attempted to feed him, disturbing other patients with his loud moaning. By 10 June he was described as less depressed and was now taking food better, but this improvement was not maintained. On 11 July he refused his food and would not respond when spoken to by staff. Although by 22 September he was eating better, he would always sit in the same chair, scarcely speaking when spoken to. In October he was thought to have 'cheered up a little', had left his old 'favourite seat' and had been seen writing a letter. He recognised that his year in the Hospital (which had started upon his admission as a voluntary boarder) was nearly up, and had asked the staff where he would be sent on discharge. This concern was thought to have 'stirred him up slightly'. On 27 November he was discharged uncured, but he did not actually leave the Hospital until 24 December 1895, by which time a transfer to Glamorgan County Lunatic Asylum at Bridgend had been arranged.

# 'Her friends have been written to repeatedly to provide clothing for her'

Taken in August 1895.

**Mary Robertson, a 43-year old governess and music teacher, living in Hampstead but originally from the Shetland Isles, was admitted from the New Hospital for Women, Euston Road on 28 April 1895.**

*She confessed to hearing voices which order her to do various acts. To seeing forms and faces, some pleasant and some horrible. To believing in these voices and faces as facts. She is greatly altered in expression of face, in manner and in type of conversation. Miss Mary Darby Sturge MB, house surgeon, New Hospital for Women, says that Mary H. Robertson is unable to concentrate her thoughts or to read because of the voices which constantly haunt her. Also she declares she has been hypnotised (which is not the case). She says that there must be electricity in the ward which acts in her.*

Dr Mary Ann Dacomb Scharlieb, New Hospital for Women, Euston Road, London

*Patient imagines herself to have been hypnotised. She declares she hears voices, and instances one as saying that her brother has been shot and also calling her by name. I am informed by Miss Mary Sturge that patient describes herself as imagining she was followed and persecuted in the streets last autumn. Also that she is alternately apathetic (with head on bed or hands over her eyes) and restless. Also that she gets out of bed continually at night declaring that voices are saying in the street that her brother is dead.*

Dr Jane Harriet Walker, New Hospital for Women, Euston Road, London

After a succession of illnesses, through which she was apparently supported by a number of families who had made her acquaintance through music lessons she gave to their children, by January 1895 Robertson had become depressed and lost interest in her friends and work. She believed that she was being pursued through the streets of London by unknown persecutors. Her condition did not improve during a six-week stay with her sister, Mrs Margaret Jamieson, at Forest Gate. Her appetite had become very poor, and she was considered to have become anaemic. Robertson had written about this to Dr Scharlieb, who had advised admission to the New Hospital for Women.

On admission to Bethlem she told the doctor that she had needed to be admitted to the Women's Hospital because of 'obstinate constipation'. She was agitated and tearful, and repeatedly asked if it was true that her brother was dead because she could hear voices saying that he had been shot. She complained to the doctor that there was electricity in her body and, to demonstrate this, would lift up one arm and then let it drop to her side. Her sleep was poor and she had to be fed with a spoon for the first few days after admission. On 5 May she was reported to be still very depressed with fits of weeping, and to be constantly asking about her mother. She continued to report that she was hearing voices. Her condition remained essentially unchanged, so that on 3 October she was described as being in a state of 'agitated depression' and would sit with her bed sheets pulled over her head, talking to herself as if answering voices. The staff appear to have become frustrated with a lack of response from her family and friends to their letters. On 20 November it was noted that, although her friends had been written to repeatedly to provide clothing for her – as at least one of them had previously promised to provide – these letters had been returned unopened. She was discharged uncured for what were described as 'special reasons' on the same day, and transferred to Essex County Lunatic Asylum at Brentwood.

## 'She didn't know which of the voices she should believe'

Taken on 7 September 1895.

**Isabella Elliott, a 29-year old housewife, was admitted from Lewisham Infirmary on 9 May 1895.**

*She is very depressed. She sits for hours gazing at the ceiling and states she is looking at visions. On several occasions, since her visit here, I have seen her in a cataleptic condition, with rigid limbs which remain for hours in any position which one may place them. Nellie Thomas, sister, 42B High Street, Lewisham, SE, states that she has for no apparent reason taken a dislike to her husband and says he is going to poison her. She will not go out because she says the people cry shame on her and say she is not married. She has catalepsy.*

Dr Frederick Sherman Toogood, Medical Superintendent, Lewisham Infirmary, High Street, Lewisham

*She sits staring vacantly out of the window. Says she is going to be shot. Says she was unhappy at home because at a concert she overheard people whispering about her shame. Her mother, Isabella Anne Thomas, 42B High Street, Lewisham, tells me that Isabella Charlotte Elliott has delusions that people are talking about her and trying to harm her.*

Dr Ernest William White Farmer, 159 High Street, Lewisham

At the time of admission she appeared very depressed and would only answer questions after they had been repeated several times. She would often burst out laughing for no apparent reason during the examination. By 13 May she was described as much improved and could now converse freely with the doctor. She told him that at a concert she had heard voices shouting out the word 'shame' to her. She was still hearing voices and was observed to turn her head to the right and left to listen to them. One voice was saying 'you are married' and the other 'you are not married'. She told the doctor that she didn't know which of the voices she should believe. She continued to believe that she was going to be shot but was unwilling to speak to the staff about this. By 3 August she was described as 'improving' and on 3 September to have lost her hallucinations and delusions. She went to Witley on 10 September, and on returning was given two months leave, which she spent, not with her family, but with friends at St Leonards-on-Sea, Sussex. Upon the Hospital's receipt of a certificate from a local doctor as to her mental state, she was discharged well on 18 December 1895.

# 'Very keen to go to Witley'

**Julia Salter, a 26-year old single woman from Lambeth, was admitted on 10 May 1895 after trying to kill her mother with a poker.**

*Was in a nervous excited condition. Stated that she intended to kill her mother and sister in order to send them to heaven and then she should take her own life in order to follow them. Said she was very wicked but could not tell anyone what she has done. Asked me to take care of her as she did not feel safe to be alone. Attempted suicide by poisoning a short time ago. William Salter, brother, 20 Webber Street, states that she has attempted to poison herself. Has cut her mother's head severely with a poker. Has also threatened her brother with a knife.*

Dr John Stonely Hill, 33 Great Charlotte Street, Blackfriars

*Has delusions saying she has two beings and is therefore not accountable for her actions. Believes she will never die and that owing to her wrongdoing, all others – her friends – will be in the same condition as herself. Says she struck her mother yesterday to send her to heaven as she (the mother) was suffering here.*

Dr John Vere Charles Denning, 174 Blackfriars Road, London

Taken in August 1895.

When examined by the admitting doctor she told him that she was unable to think of the future because her thoughts 'always went backwards' and that neither she nor anyone else could ever die. She had been wicked and because of this she injured everyone who came into contact with her. She told the doctor that she believed there ought to be a law which would allow for her to be put out of the world so that she would stop hurting those around her. On 17 May she told the doctor that she had two natures. When he asked if she could show him her other nature, she replied, 'If I did you would shut me up in a room by myself'. She remained agitated and depressed and would pace about the ward, plaiting and unplaiting her hair. By 3 August she had improved so that she was reported to be doing work around the ward and to be enjoying card puzzles. On 3 September she was described as improved, still to be playing with her hair but very keen to go to Witley. She was transferred to Witley on 9 October and was discharged well on 18 October 1896.

## 'He believed they were trying to poison him'

Taken in August 1895.

**Charles Barwick, a 41-year old clerk, was admitted from Hackney Union Infirmary, Homerton via Fisherton House, a lunatic house in Salisbury, Wiltshire, on 11 May 1895.**

*He is depressed, melancholic and suicidal. He imagines he is constantly followed about by strange people. He hears indistinct voices calling him at times. He cut his throat some short time ago.*

Dr John Joseph Gordon, Medical Superintendent, Hackney Union Infirmary, Homerton

*He is suicidal and has already attempted to cut his throat. He believes he has done something wrong whereby he is bound to be lost. He is depressed and melancholic and at times cannot take care of himself.*

Dr Alexander McDonnell, 39 Stamford Hill, Stoke Newington

He had first become depressed six months earlier and had begun to complain of headaches and that his business was going badly. In February he had cut his throat and had become very confused so that he was unable to write a letter. On 4 April he had been taken to Hackney Union Infirmary, and a week later to Fisherton House. His diagnosis on admission was melancholia and the prognosis was given as fair. He told the admitting doctor that he had been commanded by voices to cut his throat. He could no longer hear the voices and said that he now knew that they had not been real. He was very puzzled and upset by his wife, who he believed had said that she had no money, but who was dressed as usual the last time he had seen her. On 12 June he was temporarily moved to MIB ward, as he was too noisy to sleep upstairs and had refused to take a sleeping draught. He told the staff that he believed they were trying to poison him with draughts and that he would die soon. Little changed in his condition until November when he was reported to be a little brighter and to be employing himself more around the Hospital.

On 14 December a notice was served on Barwick demanding payment for money that he was said to have illegally spent from the funds of the Carlton Bank (founded 1880), of which he was a director. There is a note that all communications referring to this were sent to the patient. Later that day, Barwick was sent back down to MIB after throwing a vase at Sydney Lawford, a fellow patient, which had resulted in Lawford sustaining a lacerated head wound. Barwick claimed that Lawford had been annoying him, but this was judged not to have been the case since Lawford seldom spoke to anyone and had been standing alone at the time of the incident.

On 2 January 1896 Barwick told the doctor that he wanted to get home in order to kill one of his children. He also said that the Carlton Bank business was of no importance, and that the trouble had been started by a fellow director who had since fled the country. He remained confused and depressed, at times having to be put on observation throughout the night. He was discharged uncured on 8 April 1896. On 30 November 1897, Dr Smith received a letter from Barwick at home in Leytonstone, in which he reports his recovery and conveys his 'deep gratitude for the attention, sympathy and patience' he received at Bethlem. His recovery could not have been quite complete, however, as he reports himself unable to work, and reliant upon his wife's income, which was, he wrote, 'only just sufficient to supply our actual needs'. Nor had his grievance with the Carlton Bank been resolved. 'I am not sure if you will remember that my late employers, whom I had served faithfully and successfully for fifteen years, on the end of Christmas 1895 demanded from me between £1000 and £2000 and afterwards brought an unwarranted action for it. This greatly retarded my recovery and is, I fear, in a great measure the cause of my present infirmities, but as soon as it became likely that I should return home negotiations were commenced for a settlement and the action was ultimately abandoned by them.' The Carlton Bank went into liquidation in 1901. Of Barwick himself there is no further word.

# 'She became so difficult that her leave was withdrawn'

Taken on 6 September 1895.

**Annie Binckes, a 20-year old single woman from East Dulwich, was admitted on 11 May 1895.**

*I found her lying down, surrounded by broken crockery, her hair cut short and somewhat dishevelled in appearance. She told me she had nearly got a situation as a 'funeral' and suddenly commenced to sob on my leaving. Jane Binckes, her mother, living at the same address, informs me that she seizes her by the neck somewhat roughly. That she banged doors and broke chimney ornaments. That she cut off her own hair with a carving knife and altered her dress in an eccentric fashion.*

Dr John Rand, Glenmore, Underhill Road, Forest Hill

*Admits her violent tempers. Says she broke the china, glass, etc. to spite 'someone', 'doesn't know who' and says she is not sorry for it. Wishes to become a general servant. Is eccentric in her manner and ideas but fairly rational at time of examination. Says she 'cannot tell what she might do', referring to violent acts. The acts of violence always follow attempts at restraint. Mrs Jane Binckes, mother, same address, says 'Untruthful, eccentric in dress for three months. Very violent temper. Seized the mother violently by the hair on two occasions. Smashed all the tea things when set on the table and some ornaments – nine or ten things in all. Hides things – boots, etc. Takes keys out of doors and hides them. Put a bottle of claret up the chimney.'*

Dr Hubert Moody Wood, 261 Barry Road, Dulwich

On admission she was able to converse freely with the doctor and told him that the reason she had smashed crockery was that she had been unable to overcome a violent impulse to do this. She settled very quickly into Hospital life and on 18 May was reported to be happy and to be occupying herself by playing the piano and violin. Her improvement was not always maintained and on 22 June she became agitated, biting one of the attendants and tearing the dress of another. She began to decorate her hair with flowers taken out of her hat. In early August she became very difficult to manage, refusing to wear clothes and insisting that she had a number of physical ailments and should be supplied with crutches so that she could walk about the ward. On 3 September she was reported to be quieter but expressing beliefs that the doctors were in love with her. She asked one of them to get her an engagement ring.

Without any apparent warning she suddenly became very violent on 11 October and smashed some glasses and a washing basin on the ward and had to be restrained. She was removed to FIA ward, and had not improved by January 1896. Indeed, when the

Hospital tried to send her out for a period of leave she became so difficult that her leave was withdrawn. She continued to fail to make any improvement, was discharged uncured on 22 April 1896, and was transferred to Camberwell House, a private lunatic house in South London.

## 'Don't let my father cut my throat'

Taken in late September 1895.

**Elsie Jerrard, a 19-year old housewife from Herne Hill, was admitted on 13 May 1895.**

*She exposed herself in an indelicate way. She refused food by shutting her teeth firmly and refused to answer questions. When I saw her on 9 May she said her husband's throat was cut and spoke of people being in league with her nurse and of attempts to poison her. Robert Jerrard, 72 Shakespeare Road, Herne Hill, husband of patient, told me that he could get her to take no food or fluid. That she would not speak to him and that when she did last speak it was of cut throats, poison and conspiracies. Ellen Jerrard, 71 Knatchbull Road, mother-in-law of the patient, says that Elsie M. Jerrard said 'This is a madhouse'.*

Dr Maurice Smelt Duke, 272 Kennington Park Road, London

*The patient refused to answer any questions and stared at the ceiling the whole time. Would not put out her tongue and I had to lift or move her into any position I required to make my examination. Husband, Robert Jerrard and father, Edward Luckford, 220 Brixton Hill – patient confined one month ago. During pregnancy was very nervous and easily upset. One day some water was overturned in kitchen which upset her so much that she had to seek medical advice. A week ago she began to suspect the nurse of poisoning the child and herself. Very excitable and became odd in her manner. The excitability passed off and patient has not spoken for three days and refuses all food. Does not ask for her child which she has not seen for four days although she has suckled it up to a few days ago. Masturbation suspected.*

Dr George Frederick Hugill, Arundel Lodge, 147 Main Road, Balham

She had been brought into the Hospital on a chair and when the admitting doctor examined her he noted that she was apparently confused, lying in bed and refusing to open her mouth or speak. For the first few days she was fed by nasal tube, but by 16 May she had started to feed herself. She was nursed in a padded room and when she was allowed out of this would run about the ward, throwing herself against furniture and the walls and hitting her head against the wall so that she had to have an attendant with her at all times. She would shout out 'Don't let my father cut my throat'. On 1 June she was reported to be still intermittently very excited, shouting out and imitating the speech and actions of those around her. Treatment with hyoscine settled her, but she refused food and had to be fed by nasal tube again.

She began treatment with prolonged baths on 25 June. This commenced with an hour a day, but was gradually increased until by 3 July she was bathing for eight hours. She was reported to be 'certainly quieter' as a result of the baths but still needed to be tube-fed and would only sleep if given paraldehyde. On 9 July she was considered to be so much improved that the baths were stopped. She was now taking food, but was still described as confused and would pull her dress up or remove her clothes in front of other patients. On 15 September her behaviour worsened and she was described as 'sly and spiteful' in the notes as a result of her propensity to kick other patients from behind or when they were not looking. On 17 October and on the next three days she was isolated for up to two hours because of episodes of violence towards others.

This period of extremely challenging behaviour seems to have marked a temporary turning point in her case. A week later she was described as cheerful, tidy and orderly and almost well enough to go to Witley. She was discharged home well on 18 December 1895. However, Elsie Jerrard returned to Bethlem as a patient from 24 September 1896 to 3 October 1897, and was then discharged by transfer to the new London County Council Asylum at Claybury, which had opened in 1894. She was examined and bathed just prior to her departure and said to have 'no bruises', but she arrived at Claybury 'much bruised', according to the Lunacy Commissioners in a letter to Dr Smith dated 19 October 1897. Dr Smith provided the Commissioners with assurances concerning the state in which she left the Hospital, and information concerning the means by which she was transferred.

# 'A troubled relationship with her husband'

Taken on 7 September 1895.

**Elizabeth Dore, a 25-year old married woman from Balham, was admitted on 29 May 1895.**

*When talking she rambles from one subject to another and cannot talk for long about any subject. She hears pianos playing and other noises which do not exist. She sees and talks about persons in the room who are not present. She is sleepless and constantly wants to get out of bed. Albert Ernest Hill, Elmscroft, Melrose Road, Wandsworth, SW, brother of the patient, states patient has said that she heard the report of a pistol with which her husband was blowing his brains out and she has been rambling in her talk.*

Dr William Edwyn Falkingridge Finley, St Thomas' Hospital, Albert Embankment, London

*Great rambling of speech with evident loss of memory with regard to recent events. Incoherence of ideas. Says that she has become suspicious of all with whom she comes into contact. Has various hallucinations of sight and hearing. Talks to imaginary people. Has lately been depressed in spirits. Talks continually both day and night about the conduct of her husband and her recent confinement.*

Edward Arthur Saunders, St Thomas' Hospital, Albert Embankment, London

Her difficulties were thought to have been precipitated by a difficult pregnancy and a recent worsening of a troubled relationship with her husband. A fortnight prior to admission her husband had reportedly upset her by revealing the extent of his errant behaviour. The doctor's notes say 'He (the husband) goes in a great deal for drinking and speculating and stays away for weeks no-one knows where'. On admission she was agitated with rambling speech about her husband. She was preoccupied with his behaviour and repeatedly told staff that she had proof that he was an adulterer, and that she felt she could never again so much as shake hands with him. She also said that she could see guns and pictures on the walls of her room and could hear a voice calling 'Flo' as well as pistol shots. She refused food and had to be fed by nasal tube. On 3 July she was more rational in her conversation although she would still refuse her food, complaining that it was poisoned and tasted of gunpowder. She would mistake the identity of staff members. For example, she assured the clinical assistant, Dr Horace Pring, that they had met before at a dance in Hendon.

On 12 August she wrote to Dr Smith, asking him to prescribe her diet, sleeping hours and work patterns. 'My brain is in a very nervous state and, as I am anxious to get well quickly and go away through your kind permission, you will order the best remedies for me', she ventured. By September she began to enjoy playing the piano on the ward, and her patterns of eating and sleeping were more regular. She was transferred to Witley on 10 September, returned on 5 November and was discharged well the following day.

# 'She was kept in bed in isolation for eight hours every day'

**Jane Jones, a 40-year old housewife from Brixton, was admitted on 29 May 1895.**

*She is shrieking at the top of her voice and is so violent that she has to be held down. Makes use of bad language and exposes herself indecently. Talks utter nonsense and cannot be persuaded to be rational. Edward Oldsworth Jones, husband of patient, states that patient has been depressed for three weeks past. At midday today she suddenly became extremely violent, used abusive language and threatened to cut the throat of her child. Was controlled with great difficulty.*

Dr Seymour Graves Toller, St Thomas' Hospital, Albert Embankment, London

*Violence directed to others. Use of foul language, indecent gestures, attempts to expose private parts and incoherent manner of expression. Edward Jones informed me on my visit that his wife had expressed a desire to injure the next door neighbour and had talked about cutting one of her own children's throats.*

Dr Alexander Smith, 98 Camberwell New Road, London

Taken in late September 1895.

On admission she indecently exposed herself to the doctor and was using 'blasphemous and exceedingly disgusting language'. She was initially nursed in a gloved dress in a padded room and continued to be noisy and difficult to manage. She would throw herself around in the exercise yard and, if restraint were applied, would kick and bite the attendants. By September she was considered to have improved slightly and was noted not to be using so much bad language. But within a few weeks, things had become difficult again and she was violent. From 4 to 12 November, she was kept in bed in isolation for eight hours every day. This régime was reinstated each time she showed violence to the attendants or hurt herself by throwing herself to the ground. Unfortunately she didn't show any further improvement and had to be nursed almost continually in her room in seclusion. She was discharged uncured on 29 April 1896.

# 'She had to be strapped down on her journey to Bethlem'

Taken in late August 1895.

Katie Ashmore, a 35-year old ladies' companion from
St Ives, Huntingdonshire, was admitted on 30 May 1895.

*She talked the whole time I was present, occasionally screaming at the top of her voice. No sentence was coherent and coarse language was used such as I know from previous acquaintance with the patient she could not use in an ordinary state of mind. She requires three people always to hold her to prevent her throwing herself out of bed. She refuses her food and requires to be fed by nasal tube. Sarah Hall, of Washingly Hall, Peterborough, domestic servant, states that this patient has for four days been incoherent, noisy, requiring three or four people always with her to hold her. She has been almost entirely without sleep for six days.*

Dr William Reginald Grove, St Ives, Huntingdonshire

*She is continually talking incoherently and although sensible does not appear to have any fixed ideas or to understand what is said to her. She is occasionally violent and has to be restrained. Charles Ashton, Sheep Street, Bicester, Oxon., ironmonger, tells me that she is incessantly talking nonsense. She refuses to take any food and is obliged to be fed through a tube passed into the stomach.*

Dr William Henry Dison Mence, Ouse Villa, St Ives, Huntingdonshire

Her parents had died, within six weeks of each other, in the spring of 1895. Since her father's death she had become increasingly incoherent with more and more disturbed behaviour so that she had to be strapped down on her journey to Bethlem to prevent her from harming herself. On admission she was highly excited, talking rapidly and incoherently and throwing herself about. She tore off some of the covering from the walls of the padded room. Within a few days, although her behaviour had become quieter, she was observed to stare at the walls of her room as though she were seeing hallucinations. By 2 September, she was noted to have gained more self-control and was now able to give rational and appropriate answers to questions put to her by the staff. On 15 September she was said to be occupying herself and entertaining the other patients and was transferred to Witley on 24 September. She returned to Bethlem on 5 November and was discharged well the following day.

# 'She attacked Nurse Moody, who she said had been telling lies about her'

Taken in mid-September 1895.

**Eleanor Kennedy, a 33-year old dressmaker from Paddington, was admitted on 2 July 1895.**

*She said her mother died certainly years ago, but was not really dead as she often heard her voice distinctly. NB Her mother has been dead for 9 years. She said she disliked walking out as she could hear passers by thinking of her in a sneering and insulting manner and that they even spat upon her. Interpreted a noise in a water pipe as a spiteful assault on her boy in the next room. Lottie Stern says that the patient turns and spits upon people in the street believing that they sneered at her when in reality they have not. Also that she suspects her husband (who is most kind and devoted) of wronging and deceiving her.*

Dr William Jerman Scott, 55 Warwick Road, Paddington

*At first she would not answer any questions, then she asked me if nurses were justified in breaking patients' backs. Hers, she said, had been broken by a nurse some time ago. Says she hears voices but cannot see the people. William Kennedy, husband, says she asked him where her second child was; if in bed or not. NB The child has been dead a year or two.*

Dr Sydenham John Knott, 45 Burwood Place, Hyde Park

At admission she told the doctor that she had heard voices saying insulting and disgusting things to her for almost two years. She believed that the people whose voices she could hear were currently in her home and were ill-treating her son because she could hear his voice calling out 'Mama' to her. She had heard, she said, that boys were sometimes crucified as a punishment in schools and was afraid that this would happen to her son. She believed that it was possible that her mother had been raised from the dead because she had heard the rattling of skulls against a coffin lid. In the days following admission she would at times be impulsive and violent, throwing things at other patients and attempting to hit them. The doctor noted that she appeared to be acting at such times under the direction of voices.

On 28 July she attacked Nurse Moody, who she said had been telling lies about her. She broke a window on the ward on 2 October and had to be nursed in seclusion. By 19

November her behaviour was sufficiently improved for her to be transferred to Witley. She returned on 17 December and was granted a month's home leave the following day. Her husband, William Kennedy, wrote to Dr Smith on Monday 13 January 1896 to report her progress: 'As Mrs Kennedy will be coming to Bethlem Hospital on Wednesday, naturally you would like to know how she has been since leaving the Hospital. I must say I cannot see any cause to prevent her remaining at home. She has greatly improved and now takes an interest in home affairs.' On 15 January 1896 she was discharged well.

## 'She quickly made friends with the staff and patients in her gallery'

Taken on 10 September 1895.

Ida Schroeder, a 26-year old ladies' companion from Bayswater, was admitted on 9 July 1895.

*Incoherent answers to questions. Says that she hears people continually whispering through the wall. That Jesus Christ had appeared in the room at night. That people were continually coming in at the window to see her. Miss Florence Schroeder tells me she was found in an excitable state and talked in a rambling manner about religion and murders and had considerable difficulty in persuading her to return home.*

Dr William Frederick Parmer, 2 Linden Gardens, Bayswater

*Incoherent rambling. Asked me if I knew Horatio Nelson and if I knew Christopher Columbus. Restless and wakeful. Tossing about in the bed and picking at the bed clothes. Pupils very dilated and not easily contracting under the influence of a bright light. Miss Schroeder tells me that she found her sister in a very nervous excitable state. Stated that she felt that someone was going to murder her without any cause. Evidently influenced by an acquaintance who had committed suicide lately.*

Dr William Matthias Noott, 8 Kensington Park Road, London

On admission she answered the doctor's questions readily although he found it hard to follow her train of thought. She called Dr Horace Pring, the clinical assistant, 'Sydney Jones' (along with several other names) and told him she intended to find the murderer of Burke Godwin. She was concerned that a man known only as 'Harry' was trying to murder her. She quickly made friends with the staff and patients in her gallery, thinking that each was someone she remembered from her earlier life.

In the weeks following admission she was reported to talk almost continually, either to herself or to anyone who would converse with her in the gallery. Her behaviour could be impulsive and violent. On 27 October she broke some vases on the ward and tore her own clothes and those of other patients. She bit her fingers at the base of the nails and was fitted with padded gloves to prevent further injury. On 14 January 1896 she was reviewed and considered to be no better mentally or physically. She was reported to lie about the ward all day, refusing to help with activities and chores. Her condition remained unchanged over the following months. She was finally discharged uncured on 7 October 1896, and was transferred to St Luke's Hospital in Old Street, London.

## 'He was "stagnating" in the Hospital'

Taken in early August 1895.

**Gerard Aston, a 28-year old man from Wembley, was admitted on 16 July 1895.**

*Wildly incoherent in manner and talk. Fancies that he is about to walk to Brighton for a wager. Refuses to be controlled or reasoned with. Horace Norman of 13 Denton Road, Putney, says that he refused to go to bed at night and says he shall start at midnight for his walk to Brighton.*

Dr William Travers, 2 Phillimore Gardens, London

*Imagined he was starting for a race to Brighton at twelve that night. Was walking up and down the lawn covered with a blanket. Said he had drunk extract of alcohol and extract of beer. George Steel, attendant, says that patient represented himself as Christ. Has a desire to turn the Bishop of London out of his palace and threatens to murder people.*

Dr Frederick Heales Carter, 99 Upper Richmond Road, Putney

A week before admission he had begun to talk to his landlady in the kitchen, something he would not have done when well. He had then begun to insist that he took his breakfast in the garden and talked a great deal about walking to Brighton. He became restless, excited and over-talkative and had two attendants to look after him at home. He had sent a telegram to his bookmaker which he had signed 'The Champion Fifty-Mile Walker'. His admission diagnosis was acute mania and his prognosis was given as good.

Following admission he continued to express the belief that he was God, and the Son of God. He developed inflammation of the penis, which was treated with Boracic fomentations, but because he would not leave the dressings alone he was made to wear padded gloves. From 9 to 16 October he wore the gloves for twenty-two hours a day.

On 1 January 1896 he was described as steadily improving and was now in one of the upper galleries. On 28 January 1896 he was transferred to Witley, and returned much improved to Bethlem on 2 June. The next day he was considered to still look somewhat depressed but not to be suicidal or a risk to himself in any way. He was 'stagnating' in the Hospital and the physician considered he would probably be better if tried out at home. He was given three months leave of absence on 3 June. On the same afternoon, he asked Dr Smith, the Physician Superintendent, if he could go out of the Hospital for two hours to see his Uncle who lived at Dean's Yard, Westminster. He left with Dr Smith's permission, but did not return to the Hospital. His friends were all contacted, but none of them had seen the patient or knew of his whereabouts. On the following day, the police were alerted to his disappearance.

On 7 June, Dr Smith heard from the police that a body had been found in the Thames just below Teddington Lock. William Slattery, the head attendant, was sent out and identified it as that of the patient. At the inquest on 10 June the verdict was 'found drowned'.

## 'A Hospital friendship'

Taken in August 1895.

Hermann Müller, known to his friends as 'the Doc', a 52-year old German teacher who had admitted himself as a voluntary boarder at Bethlem on 22 June 1895, was admitted as a certified patient on 30 July 1895. Born in Germany, he earned a doctorate at the University of Berlin before emigrating to England at the age of twenty-five and taking up work as a schoolteacher, first at Darlington, then, from 1890, at Whitgift School, Croydon. He had previously been an inpatient at Bethlem from 13 August 1892 to 30 March 1893.

*Patient states that he was in Bethlem Hospital three years ago. Says that lately he has been very much depressed owing to his being constantly under the impression that someone was following him. Has frequently heard the voices of his friends conversing with him. Has been unable to sleep and unable to take his food. William Riddaway, Bethlem attendant, says the patient imagines he is being 'shadowed'. He is noisy at night and refuses his food. Neither washes nor dresses himself. Is also under the impression that a patient is taking liberties with him.*

Dr Seymour Graves Toller, St Thomas' Hospital, Albert Embankment, London

*Patient is very garrulous. He tells me he has just been sent back from the convalescent home at Witley as he was so restless and noisy. That he does not know if he was hypnotised. He thinks at times he is shadowed and followed and that one of the patients at Witley was desirous of committing an unnatural offence on him. That he hears bangings and hammerings and he thinks at times voices. William Riddaway, Bethlem attendant, tells me patient is restless, stands gazing about the gallery, stamping at times, noisy at nights, has to be made to wash and dress himself, does not occupy himself.*

Dr William Francis Umney, 15 Crystal Palace Park Road, Sydenham

Following certification and admission, details of his behaviour during his three weeks at Witley as a voluntary boarder emerged. He had believed that people were 'shadowing' him if they moved their arms and hands in a particular way. He had seen a fellow patient in the bath and believed that this man had suggested that they should commit an 'unnatural offence' together. Indeed, immediately prior to his voluntary admission on 22 June, he had visited the Hospital several times in a state of anxiety over what he recognised to be delusions about being the subject of unwelcome homosexual advances. 'There had just been a good deal of excitement over the Oscar Wilde case,' observed the admitting doctor drily. Müller's admission diagnosis was acute mania and the prognosis was given as fair.

His behaviour continued to cause concern and he was described as 'destructive and mischievous', engaging in scuffles with the attendants, who he believed were working against him, in particular the head attendant William Slattery. On 18 January 1896 he told Dr Hyslop, the senior assistant medical officer, of his belief that he was not properly informed on admission of his right to see a magistrate and that he had been given the wrong notices about this at the time. He was shown the counterfoils from his admission certificates and notices, but was not convinced by them. On 24 January he told the doctor that a person had visited the Hospital on the previous day in the guise of Mr Bagot, a Commissioner in Lunacy, but that he had really been Professor Friedrich Max Müller of Oxford (no relation to Hermann Müller), to whom he – Hermann – had written in 1892. He also claimed that the Hospital was 'one mass of delusions and frauds' and that the staff would make suggestions to him that he was unable to resist. This was the cause, he said, of some of his earlier destructive and violent behaviour. He said that he believed that the staff tried to make certain of the patients worse and that he was one of them.

Through the spring of 1896 he showed very little improvement, remaining suspicious and having to be fed by tube. On 6 June there is a note that he was greatly improved, now reading and usefully employing himself. Also, all his ideas about 'planets and suggestion' had left him. This improvement was maintained and he went to Witley on 25 August. He returned well from Witley on 20 October and was given home leave. He returned every month to be reviewed by the doctor. When he was seen on 3 January 1897, he was found to be in a confused mental state. He was detained at the Hospital, and a wire was sent to his wife informing her of this. By 13 January, Dr Smith, the Physician Superintendent, had decided that Müller seemed 'unlikely to recover sufficiently to resume work or live at home'. Burdened with the support and education of their two children, aged twelve and fourteen respectively, his wife was 'quite unable to pay for her husband in any asylum'. Yet her husband was judged 'a man of great culture and would feel most acutely the association with the pauper class in a county asylum'. Accordingly Dr Smith recommended him as suitable for transfer to Bethlem's incurable ward. On 28 January, Müller was still very confused, believing that the world may be overbalanced at any time. On 3 March 1897 he was sent to the incurable ward.

An intriguing postscript to the medical records of this patient is provided by the report of his death, which occurred three days short of his seventy-third birthday. In the March 1916 issue of the Hospital magazine *Under the Dome*, Geoffrey O'Donoghue, Hospital chaplain, wrote 'It was my sad privilege ... to say the last prayers and breathe a long farewell over the oldest of my friends in the Hospital'. He went on to record, 'In his best years he was my constant companion and very valuable amanuensis. I imagine that he originally owed to me his love of perambulating

Taken sometime in 1900.

London in search of the historical and curious. But I am sure that I first took with him the invigorating and picturesque walks among the Surrey hills, which I now take alone. In my early studies of the documents upon which my *Story of Bethlehem Hospital* was founded, I was under the greatest obligations to his knowledge of languages, his accurate scholarship and the neatness of his handwriting. So much said – and much left unsaid – to the memory of a Hospital friendship.'

Following Hermann Müller's death, his son, H. Eric Miller – his surname altered so as not to offend British wartime sensibilities – wrote to the Governors of Bethlem Hospital to express the gratitude of the family for the care given to his father. 'The generous reception which was accorded my father when he broke down in 1895 certainly enabled my mother to fight the battles of life on behalf of her children and herself in a manner which would not have been possible had my father been in less hospitable hands', he wrote. Subsequently the 'Miller Relief Fund' was established, from a £1000 donation made by Eric Miller, towards the support of Bethlem patients' families, and for the support of convalescent patients recently discharged from the Hospital. It continues in use today as a hardship fund. Upon hearing of the proposed donation, the new Physician Superintendent wrote to Mr Miller in 1916, 'I know your father could not have wished anything better than to have given something to the ancient foundation where he spent so many years of his life in peace and, I think, happiness'.